NEW 2018

BY ARGO BROTHERS

COMMON CORE MATH

GRADE 6

PART II: FREE RESPONSE

Visit **www.argoprep.com** to get
FREE access to our online platform.

1000+ Minutes of Video Explanations and more!

Authors:	Kellie Zimmer
	Anayet Chowdhury
	Eduard Suleyman
	Vladislav Suleyman
Design:	Vladislav Suleyman

At Argo Brothers, we are dedicated to providing quality and effective supplemental practice for your child. We would love to hear your honest feedback and **review** of our workbooks on **Amazon**.

Argo Brothers is one of the leading providers of supplemental educational products and services. We offer affordable and effective test prep solutions to educators, parents and students. Learning should be fun and easy! For that reason, most of our workbooks come with detailed video answer explanations taught by one of our fabulous instructors. Our goal is to make your life easier, so let us know how we can help you by e-mailing us at **info@argobrothers.com.**

ISBN: 978-0997994896
Published by Argo Brothers, Inc.

OTHER BOOKS BY ARGO BROTHERS

Here are some other test prep workbooks by Argo Brothers you may be interested in. All of our workbooks come equipped with detailed video explanations to make your learning experience a breeze! Subscribe to our mailing list at www.argobrothers.com to receive custom updates about your education.

GRADE 2

GRADE 3

GRADE 4

GRADE 5

GRADE 6

GRADE 7

GRADE 4

GRADE 5

TABLE OF
CONTENTS

HOW TO USE THE BOOK

This workbook is designed to give lots of practice with the math Common Core State Standards (CCSS). By practicing and mastering this entire workbook, your child will become very familiar and comfortable with the state math exam. If you are a teacher using this workbook for your student's, you will notice each question is labeled with the specific standard so you can easily assign your students problems in the workbook. This workbook takes the CCSS and divides them up among 20 weeks. By working on these problems on a daily basis, students will be able to (1) find any deficiencies in their understanding and/or practice of math and (2) have small successes each day that will build proficiency and confidence in their abilities.

You can find detailed video explanations to each problem in the book by visiting:
www.argoprep.com

We strongly recommend watching the videos as it will reinforce the fundamental concepts. Please note, scrap paper may be necessary while using this workbook so that the student has sufficient space to show their work.

For a detailed overview of the Common Core State Standards for 6th grade, please visit:
www.corestandards.org/Math/Content/6/introduction/

For more practice with 6th Grade Math, be sure to check out our other book, Common Core Math Workbook Grade 6: Multiple Choice

You want to become better at math and that process will start now. This week you will practice dividing with fractions, solving word problems and using models to represent problems.

You can find detailed video explanations to each problem in the book by visiting:
ArgoPrep.com

---

1. The area of an athletic field is $\frac{3}{16}$ square kilometers. The length of the field is $\frac{3}{8}$ kilometer. What is the width, in km, of the field?

6.NS.1

---

2. The carpet runner was $4\frac{1}{8}$ square yards. If the remnant was $\frac{3}{4}$ yards wide, what was its length?

6.NS.1

---

3. How many cups of pudding would 3 people get if they equally shared $\frac{2}{3}$ cup of pudding?

6.NS.1

---

4. How many $\frac{1}{4}$ - cup servings are in $3\frac{1}{2}$ cups of espresso?

6.NS.1

---

5. Write an expression for the model below.

$6\frac{1}{4}$								
$\frac{3}{4}$	$\frac{3}{4}$	$\frac{3}{4}$	$\frac{3}{4}$	$\frac{3}{4}$	$\frac{3}{4}$	$\frac{3}{4}$	$\frac{3}{4}$	$\frac{1}{4}$

6.NS.1

---

6. How wide is a rectangular strip of sod that is $\frac{3}{4}$ - yard long and has an area of $\frac{1}{3}$ square yards?

6.NS.1

---

1. The area of a rectangular Zen garden is $\frac{7}{12}$ square kilometers. The length of the garden is $\frac{2}{3}$ kilometer. What is the width, in km, of the garden?

6.NS.1

---

2. How many $\frac{1}{3}$ - cup servings are in $12\frac{4}{6}$ cups of juice?

6.NS.1

---

3. The length of a board is $\frac{4}{5}$ meters. If the area of the board is $\frac{8}{15}$ square meters, what is the width of the board?

6.NS.1

---

4. Write an expression for the diagram below.

$5\frac{1}{4}$										
$\frac{1}{2}$	$\frac{1}{2}$	$\frac{1}{2}$	$\frac{1}{2}$	$\frac{1}{2}$	$\frac{1}{2}$	$\frac{1}{2}$	$\frac{1}{2}$	$\frac{1}{2}$	$\frac{1}{2}$	$\frac{1}{4}$

6.NS.1

---

5. What is the value of $\frac{7}{8} \div \frac{11}{12}$?

6.NS.1

---

6. How many cups of ketchup would 13 hamburgers get if there was $3\frac{1}{4}$ cups of ketchup to be equally split among the 13 burgers?

6.NS.1

DAY 3

There are 5 fifths in one whole.

---

1. Write an expression for the diagram below.

$2\frac{5}{6}$								
$\frac{1}{3}$	$\frac{1}{3}$	$\frac{1}{3}$	$\frac{1}{3}$	$\frac{1}{3}$	$\frac{1}{3}$	$\frac{1}{3}$	$\frac{1}{3}$	$\frac{1}{6}$

6.NS.1

---

2. The length of a rectangular flag is $\frac{2}{3}$ meter. If the area of the flag is $\frac{1}{2}$ square meter, what is the width of the flag?

6.NS.1

---

3. There are 5 sisters who are to share 11 dollars. How many dollars will each sister get?

6.NS.1

---

4. The length of a counter is $\frac{1}{3}$ - yard. If the area of the counter is $\frac{4}{15}$ square yards, what is the width of the counter?

6.NS.1

---

5. The length of a picture is $3\frac{1}{3}$ inches. If the area of the picture is $7\frac{1}{2}$ square inches, what is the width of the photograph?

6.NS.1

---

6. How many fourths are in $\frac{7}{8}$?

6.NS.1

---

1. The race is $9\frac{1}{3}$ miles long and each runner will run $\frac{1}{4}$ of the race. How far will each runner run?

6.NS.1

---

2. How many $\frac{1}{3}$ - cup servings are in $3\frac{1}{2}$ cups of coffee?

6.NS.1

---

3. There are $10\frac{1}{2}$ cookies. If Anastasia, Bella and Cali share them equally, how many cookies will each girl receive?

6.NS.1

---

4. The area of the science lab was $310\frac{4}{5}$ square meters. If the width is $18\frac{1}{2}$ meters, what is the length, in meters, of the lab?

6.NS.1

---

5. Write an expression for the model below.

$4\frac{1}{2}$						
$\frac{2}{3}$	$\frac{2}{3}$	$\frac{2}{3}$	$\frac{2}{3}$	$\frac{2}{3}$	$\frac{2}{3}$	$\frac{1}{2}$

6.NS.1

---

6. How many $\frac{1}{8}$ - gallon servings are in 8 gallons?

6.NS.1

DAY 5 ASSESSMENT

1. How many thirds are in $5\frac{4}{6}$?

6.NS.1

2. The length of a briefcase is $18\frac{1}{2}$ inches. If the area of the case is $249\frac{3}{4}$ square inches, what is the width of the briefcase?

6.NS.1

3. The stage was $11\frac{1}{3}$ yards wide and had an area of 119 square yards. What is the length of the stage?

6.NS.1

4. Write an expression modeled by the diagram below.

$3\frac{1}{4}$						
$\frac{1}{2}$	$\frac{1}{2}$	$\frac{1}{2}$	$\frac{1}{2}$	$\frac{1}{2}$	$\frac{1}{2}$	$\frac{1}{4}$

6.NS.1

5. How many $\frac{1}{6}$-gallons are in $4\frac{2}{3}$ gallons?

6.NS.1

6. The ribbon was $3\frac{1}{4}$ inches wide and had an area of $19\frac{1}{2}$ square inches. What is the length of the ribbon?

6.NS.1

DAY 6
CHALLENGE QUESTION

How many sixths are in two and one-half?

6.NS.1

WEEK 2

ARGOPREP.COM

VIDEO EXPLANATIONS

In Week 2 you will get lots of practice dividing multi-digit numbers as well as adding, subtracting, multiplying and dividing decimal numbers.

You can find detailed video explanations to each problem in the book by visiting:
ArgoPrep.com

DAY 1

When dividing, if the divisor does not go into a number at least once, please make sure to use a zero to hold the place.

1. What is the quotient of 3,536 and 17?

6.NS.2

2. There were 752 chairs that needed to be placed evenly into 36 rows. What is the smallest number of chairs each row would have?

6.NS.2

3. What is 1,752 ÷ 25? (Leave answer with a remainder.)

6.NS.2

4. The rope was 198 feet long. If each piece was cut so that it was 7 feet long, how many 7-foot pieces could be made from the rope?

6.NS.2

5. Adam shared his 147 toy cars evenly among 7 friends. How many cars did Adam give each friend?

6.NS.2

6. How many $\frac{1}{4}$ - cup servings are in $6\frac{1}{2}$ cups of egg nog?

6.NS.1

TIP of the **DAY**

When reading a word problem, if it says that something will be shared evenly, that indicates there is division involved.

DAY 2

1. What is 4,662 ÷ 14?

6.NS.2

2. What is the quotient of 5,078 and 29? (Leave answer with a remainder.)

6.NS.2

3. Ansley baked 159 muffins for the bake sale. Each container holds 6 muffins. How many containers would she need if she bagged ALL of the muffins?

6.NS.2

4. The length of a carry-on piece of luggage is $20\frac{1}{2}$ inches. If the area of the carry-on is $240\frac{7}{8}$ square inches, what is the width of the carry-on?

6.NS.1

5. Alex had 2,180 candles that he needed to ship. He could only put 36 candles in a box. How many FULL boxes would Alex have?

6.NS.2

6. There were 4,105 golf balls that were be to be placed into 37 buckets. If each bucket received the exact same number of golf balls, how many golf balls would NOT be able to be placed in a bucket?

6.NS.2

 **DAY 3**

When dividing by a decimal number, remember that you move the decimal point as many places as necessary to obtain a whole number. (You also must move the decimal point the same number of places in the dividend as well.)

 **TIP** of the **DAY**

---

1. Alicia had 62 headbands. If she kept them on 8 ribbons, what was the average number of headbands per ribbon? Round your answer to the nearest hundredth.

6.NS.3

---

2. The first piece of yarn was 18.6 cm long. The second piece of yarn was 2.3 times as long as the first piece. How long was the second piece?

6.NS.3

---

3. Alise was saving money for a new phone. She had $47 in her account when she received $54.29 for her birthday. She then spent $30.01 on some clothes. How much money does Alise have available for her phone?

6.NS.3

---

4. Andrea had 12 yards of ribbon and each bow required 2.6 yards. How many complete bows can Andrea make with her ribbon?

6.NS.3

---

5. What is the solution of the equation below?

$y - 4.7 = 18.6$

6.NS.3

---

6. Aiden went biking for 1,176 kilometers. If he rode the same distance each day and the trip took him 14 days, how far did Aiden bike each day?

6.NS.2

When answering word problems, check for key words that can tell you whether to use addition, subtraction, multiplication and/or division.

DAY 4

---

1. Charles had 42.3 feet of twine to tie off some packages. He used 6.6 feet on 4 packages and 7.5 on another package. How much twine did Charles have left?

6.NS.3

---

2. Five families had 25.9 pounds of oranges to share. How many pounds of oranges would each family get?

6.NS.3

The chart below shows the distance that 4 people drove for vacation.
Use the information to answer questions 3 – 5.

Student	Distance (mi)
Alfie	412.8
Brendon	370.5
Charity	604.3
Devon	592

---

3. How much farther did Alfie drive than Brendon?

6.NS.3

---

4. How much farther did Devon drive than Brendon?

6.NS.3

---

5. What is the total distance the 4 people drove?

6.NS.3

DAY 5 ASSESSMENT

1. What is 6,732 ÷ 17?

6.NS.2

2. Celeste packed 12 pairs of shoes in each box. If she had 388 pairs of shoes to package, how many full boxes would she have?

6.NS.2

3. The length of a roof is $8\frac{1}{3}$ meters. If the area of the roof is $45\frac{5}{6}$ square meters, what is the width of the roof?

6.NS.1

4. There are 9 puppies. If they all average 3.8 pounds, what is the total weight of all 9 puppies?

6.NS.3

5. Blaine used 8.7 gallons of gas for his trip. Brenda uses 1.9 times that amount. How much gas does Brenda use? Round your answer to the nearest tenth.

6.NS.3

6. Last month Benny had to drive 6,420 miles for work. If there were 30 days last month and he drove the same number of miles each day, how many miles did Benny drive each day?

6.NS.2

DAY 6
CHALLENGE
QUESTION

Calista was 24.8 inches tall. Her mom was 2.2 times that height and her aunt was $8\frac{3}{4}$ inches taller than Calista's mom. How tall was Calista's aunt? Round your answer to the nearest inch.

6.NS.3

Week 3 is fun! You can find the GCF (greatest common factor) and LCM (least common multiple) among 2 or 3 numbers. You will also begin using positive and negative numbers, which are helpful in real life – banking, hiking, temperatures and more!

You can find detailed video explanations to each problem in the book by visiting: ArgoPrep.com

DAY 1

The GCF is the Greatest Common Factor and it is the largest number two of its multiples have in common.

1. What is the greatest common factor of 46 and 23?

6.NS.4

2. What is the least common multiple of 12 and 8?

6.NS.4

Below is a schedule of how often 3 bus lines can complete their routes. All routes start at the Main East stop. **Use the information to answer questions 3 – 4.**

Line	Route Time
Green	10 minutes
Yellow	18 minutes
Orange	15 minutes

3. If the Green and Orange lines leave Main East at the same time and run continuously, how long before they would leave Main East at the same time?

6.NS.4

4. If the Orange and Yellow lines leave Main East at the same time and run continuously, how long before they would leave Main East at the same time?

6.NS.4

5. Connor can draw a picture in 4 minutes and Colin can draw a picture in 5 minutes. If they start drawing at the same time and draw continuously, how many minutes until they will both be finished drawing?

6.NS.4

1. What is the greatest common factor of 50 and 75?

6.NS.4

2. How many $\frac{1}{2}$ - cup servings are in $2\frac{3}{4}$ cups of ice cream?

6.NS.1

3. The trip from Exeter to Springly and back takes 12 hours by bike and 8 hours by car. If the drivers and riders could keep moving constantly, how many hours would it be before the biker and driver left Exeter at the same time?

6.NS.4

4. What is the greatest common factor of 49 and 56?

6.NS.4

5. Each box contains 5 cans of tomatoes and 2 bags of oranges. If a can of tomatoes weighs 1.7 pounds and a bag of oranges weighs 8.2 pounds, what is the combined weight of 2 boxes?

6.NS.3

6. What is the least common multiple of 9 and 12?

6.NS.4

1. The rain gauge measures 5.1 centimeters. How would the water level need to change so that the gauge measured 0 centimeters?

6.NS.5

2. Chelsea had a bank balance of - $143.78. What would she need to do get a zero balance?

6.NS.5

3. Cliff had $512 in his account. How much can he withdraw so that he has a zero balance?

6.NS.5

4. What is the least common multiple of 4 and 11?

6.NS.4

5. What is the greatest common factor of 66 and 99?

6.NS.4

6. The length of a blanket is $7\frac{3}{4}$ feet. If the area of the blanket is $34\frac{1}{10}$ square feet, what is the width of the blanket?

6.NS.1

1. The temperature is – 4.7°C. How would the temperature need to change so that the temperature is 0°C.

6.NS.5

2. Bess is at 615 meters above sea level. How many meters should he travel to reach sea level?

6.NS.5

3. Write an addition expression that is equivalent to 7 (4 + 2).

6.NS.4

4. What is the value of *t* in the equation below?

$71.3 - y = 0$

6.NS.5

5. What is the least common multiple of 6 and 7?

6.NS.4

6. Duane owed $591.08 to the credit card company. How much should he pay so that he no longer owes the credit card company any money?

6.NS.5

1. What is the value of *m* in the equation below?

$m + 91.3 = 0$

6.NS.5

2. The Mulligans take a trip from Louven to Kekoskee and back. Their trip takes 4 days. The Bakers leave at the same time to make the same trip but it takes them 5 days. If the Mulligans and the Bakers continue to make the trips, how many days will it be before they are both leaving Louven again at the same time?

6.NS.4

3. Carsten was at 702 feet below sea level then he traveled – 194 feet. How many feet should he travel to reach sea level?

6.NS.5

4. What is the GCF of 12, 18 and 24?

6.NS.4

5. Bart charged $219 to buy a suit and then he charged $72 for shoes. How can he get his credit card account back down to a zero balance?

6.NS.5

6. What is the least common multiple of 5, 9 and 18?

6.NS.4

DAY 6
CHALLENGE
QUESTION

Calvin was located at 955 yards above sea level when he moved down 150 yards to get near water. He then increased his altitude by 800 yards. What altitude will Calvin have to travel to get back to sea level? 6.NS.5

This week we will look at numbers and see where they lie on a number line. You will also get practice using TWO number lines at the same time. These 2 axes form the rectangular coordinate system.

You can find detailed video explanations to each problem in the book by visiting:
ArgoPrep.com

The origin has coordinates (0, 0) and is located where the x and y axes intersect.

Use the coordinate system below to answer questions 1 – 5.

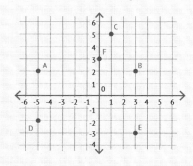

1. What is the y-coordinate of Point E?

6.NS.6

2. What point is located at (−5, 2)?

6.NS.6

3. How many units are between the origin and Point F?

6.NS.6

4. What are the coordinates for Point C?

6.NS.6

5. What quadrant would the point with the coordinates (4, -1) be in?

6.NS.6

6. Davida has 5,608 beans and she wants to make bean bags that each contain 48 beans. How many full bags will she have?

6.NS.2

When looking at information on a rectangular coordinate system, be sure to understand the labels for units and the axes.

DAY 2

Use the coordinate system below to answer questions 1 – 5.

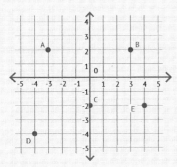

1. Write a statement that describes the relationship between Point A and Point B.

6.NS.6

2. What is the distance between Points C and E?

6.NS.6

3. What is the x-coordinate for Point D?

6.NS.6

4. What are the coordinates for Point C?

6.NS.6

5. What quadrant would the point located at (-0.2, 3.1) be in?

6.NS.6

6. Point K is located at (3, -5). Point L is a reflection of Point K, reflected across the x-axis. What are the coordinates of Point L?

6.NS.6

 **DAY 3**

Absolute value is a distance and is always positive. The absolute value of a number is the number's distance from zero.

 **TIP** of the **DAY**

Deanne is a hiker and she recorded her altitude at 5 different points of her hike. Those results are shown below. **Use this information to answer questions 1 – 4.**

Recording	Altitude (feet)
#1	508
#2	-2,167
#3	2,098
#4	-1,966
#5	2,106

1. If Deanne wants to plot the altitudes on a number line, which record will be the furthest to the left on the number line?

6.NS.7

2. At which record was she the highest altitude above sea level?

6.NS.7

3. Which record has the largest absolute value?

6.NS.7

4. Write an inequality that compares the altitudes for records #4 and #5.

6.NS.7

5. The length of Cassidy's bed comforter is $9\frac{1}{4}$ feet. If the area of the comforter is $69\frac{3}{8}$ square feet, what is the width of the comforter?

6.NS.1

---

1. Write a true inequality using |−11| and −7.

6.NS.7

Use the following set of numbers to answer questions 2 – 4.

$|-\frac{1}{4}|$, −3, |−5|, |2|, 0.4

---

2. Which number lies furthest to the left on the number line?

6.NS.7

---

3. Which number has the largest value?

6.NS.7

---

4. Which number's opposite is positive?

6.NS.7

---

5. What is 9108 ÷ 23?

6.NS.2

---

6. Which expression is modeled by the diagram below?

$4\frac{3}{4}$

$\frac{1}{2}$	$\frac{1}{2}$	$\frac{1}{2}$	$\frac{1}{2}$	$\frac{1}{2}$	$\frac{1}{2}$	$\frac{1}{2}$	$\frac{1}{2}$	$\frac{1}{2}$	$\frac{1}{4}$

6.NS.1

DAY 5 ASSESSMENT

Use the rectangular coordinate system below to answer questions 1 – 3.

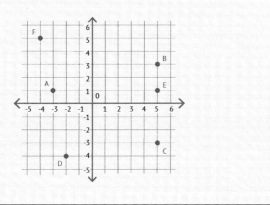

1. Which point has the coordinates (-4, 5)?

6.NS.6

2. What are the coordinates of Point D?

6.NS.6

3. Which point is a reflection of Point B across the x-axis?

6.NS.6

4. Using the numbers − 5.8 and $|-\frac{14}{3}|$, write a true inequality.

6.NS.7

Use the following set of numbers to answer questions 5 – 6.

$A = |-2.6|$, $B = 1.9$, $C = |-\frac{2}{3}|$, $D = -4$, and $E = |0.8|$

5. Which letter shows a value that is the opposite of − 0.8?

6.NS.7

6. If the letters above were placed on a number line based on their values, how would the letters be arranged from left to right on the number line?

6.NS.7

DAY 6
CHALLENGE QUESTION

Point P is located at (-2, -5). Point Q is a reflection of Point P, reflected across the y-axis. What quadrant is Point Q in?

6.NS.6

This week you will get to graph points that represent real numbers in real situations. You will also be able to name the ordered pair that shows the location of a point. Have you ever wondered what an exponent is? Week 5 you will also learn how to write and evaluate numbers that involve exponents.

You can find detailed video explanations to each problem in the book by visiting:
ArgoPrep.com

DAY 1

The distance of anything is always a positive number. Even though a car may travel in reverse, the distance traveled is still positive.

1. The coordinates of the vertices of a rectangle are A (-8, 2), B (-8, -1), C (3, -1) and D (3, 2). What are the dimensions of the rectangle?

6.NS.8

2. What are the coordinates of the line segments' endpoints below?

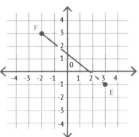

6.NS.8

Use the rectangular coordinate system and the parallelogram shown below to answer questions 3 – 4.

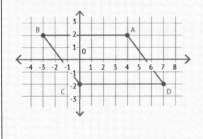

3. What is the distance of Line Segment AB?

6.NS.8

4. What is the distance of Line Segment CD?

6.NS.8

The coordinates of the vertices of a rectangle are A (-2, 4), B (-2, -1), C (4, -1) and D (4, 4).
Use this information to answer questions 5 – 6.

5. What are the dimensions of the rectangle?

6.NS.8

6. What is the length of Line Segment BC?

6.NS.8

If a line segment has x-coordinates that are the same, you can find the distance by finding the absolute value of the difference between the y-coordinates, $d = |y_2 - y_1|$

DAY 2

---

1. The coordinates of the vertices of a rectangle are A (4, 6), B (4, -1), C (0, -1) and D (0, 6). What are the dimensions of the rectangle?

6.NS.8

---

2. What is the greatest common factor of 32 and 72?

6.NS.4

---

3. A line segment is shown below. What are the coordinates of the endpoints?

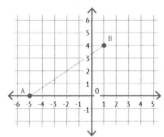

6.NS.8

The coordinates of the vertices of a rectangle are A (2, 3), B (2, -5), C (-2, -5) and D (-2, 3). These coordinates represent a square of material. **Use this information to answer questions 4 – 5.**

---

4. What are the dimensions of the rectangle?

6.NS.8

---

5. What is the area of the rectangle?

6.NS.8

---

6. What is the least common multiple of 6 and 8?

6.NS.4

DAY 3

When finding the value of expressions, be sure to find the value of the exponential numbers before adding or subtracting.

TIP of the DAY

---

1. What is the value of the expression below?

$$6^3 - 13$$

6.EE.1

---

2. What is the value of the expression below?

$$8 + 2^4$$

6.EE.1

---

3. What is the value of the expression below?

$$4^2 + \frac{2}{3}(6^2 - 3^2)$$

6.EE.1

---

4. What is the value of the expression below?

$$22 + 13^2 \times 5$$

6.EE.1

---

5. What is the value of the expression below?

$$21\frac{1}{2} - 2^4 \times (3\frac{1}{3} + 5\frac{4}{6})$$

6.EE.1

---

6. Claudia and Claire are walking around the park. It takes Claudia 12 minutes to complete a loop and it takes Claire 8 minutes to make the same loop. If they start at the same spot and continue walking at a consistent speed, how many minutes will it be until Claudia and Claire are both back at their starting point?

6.NS.4

DAY 4

1. What is the value of the expression below?

$5^4 + 263$

6.EE.1

2. What is the value of the expression below?

$20 - 4^3$

6.EE.1

3. What is the value of the expression below?

$5^3 - \frac{2}{5}(86 - 2^4)$

6.EE.1

4. What is the value of the expression below?

$335 - 7^2 \times 3$

6.EE.1

5. What is the value of -4^4 ?

6.EE.1

6. What is the value of the expression below?

$209\frac{3}{4} - 3^2 \times \left(8^2 - 38\frac{1}{2}\right)$

6.EE.1

There is a quadrilateral with the following vertices: A (-3,-4), B (-3, 2), C (1, 2) and D (1,-4).
Use this information to answer questions 1 – 3.

1. What is the length of Line Segment CD?

6.NS.8

2. What is the length of Line Segment AD?

6.NS.8

3. What is the area of the quadrilateral?

6.NS.8

4. What is the value of -2^5?

6.EE.1

5. What is the value of the expression below?

$$61 \tfrac{4}{5} - 4^2 \times \left(8 \tfrac{1}{2} - 5^2 \right)$$

6.EE.1

6. What is the value of g in the equation below?

$$14.29 + g = 0$$

6.NS.5

DAY 6
CHALLENGE
QUESTION

What is the value of the expression below?

$$(-1)^5 - 9^2$$

6.EE.1

36

WEEK 6

ARGOPREP.COM

VIDEO EXPLANATIONS

Week 6 you can practice finding if numbers are solutions to equations. Simply substitute in the number, do the operations and if it matches, you have a solution!

You can find detailed video explanations to each problem in the book by visiting:
ArgoPrep.com

To find the value of an equation that has a variable, replace the variable with its value and simplify the equation.

---

1. What is the value of the expression below if $z = 2$?

$z^5 - 3z$

6.EE.2

---

2. What is the value of the expression below when $a = 4$ and $b = -5$?

$5a - 3b$

6.EE.2

---

3. What is the value of the expression below when $m = -4$ and $n = -10$?

$-8m - n$

6.EE.2

---

4. What is the value of the expression below when $r = \frac{1}{4}$ and $s = -3$?

$-28r - 12s - 8$

6.EE.2

Use the coordinate system below to answer questions 5 – 6.

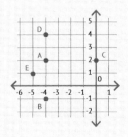

---

5. What are the coordinates for Point C?

6.NS.6

---

6. What point is located 5 units from Point B?

6.NS.6

Some students are afraid of variables. Variables are just holding a place in an equation until we can find the missing number.

DAY 2

1. What is the value of the expression below if a = − 8?

$-2a + 14$

6.EE.2

2. What is the value of the expression below when $f = -2$ and $g = 7$?

$3f + 4g - 13$

6.EE.2

3. What is the value of the expression below when $x = 5$ and $y = -2$?

$7x - y^5 + 8$

6.EE.2

4. What is the value of the expression below when $c = 9$ and $d = -10$?

$-5c + d$

6.EE.2

5. Write a true inequality that compares $|-\frac{5}{6}|$ and $-|-\frac{5}{6}|$.

6.NS.7

6. In which quadrant would (-4.1, -2) be located?

6.NS.6

 **DAY 3**

When a variable has an exponent, only the value of the variable is being squared, cubed, etc. For example, $-k^2$; $k = 3$ means $-k^2 = -(3)(3) = -9$ NOT $(-3)(-3)$

 **TIP** of the **DAY**

---

1. What is the value of the expression below if $k = 5$?

$-k^2 + 3k - 11$

6.EE.2

---

2. What is the value of the expression below when h = −4.5 and $f = 8$?

$-2h - 3.1f$

6.EE.2

---

3. What is the value of the expression below when $p = -4$ and $q = 7$?

$9p - q^2 + 16$

6.EE.2

Ava took 5 tests and she earned an 85 on the first test. The next 4 test scores are shown below in relation to her first test score. **Use this information to answer questions 4 – 5.**

Test	Score (points)
#2	− 5
#3	+ 7
#4	+ 2
#5	− 9

---

4. If Ava's scores were plotted on a number line, which test would be the furthest to the left on that number line?

6.NS.7

---

5. Write a true inequality comparing Tests #2 and #5.

6.NS.7

1. Write an expression that is equivalent to $7(y - 8)$.

6.EE.3

2. Write an expression that has the same value as $d + d + d + d$.

6.EE.3

3. Use the Distributive Property to expand $10(5f - 3g)$.

6.EE.3

4. What is another way to write $8b + a + 11 - a + 4b$?

6.EE.3

5. Point U is located at (-3, 4). Point V is a reflection of Point U, reflected across the y-axis. What are the coordinates of Point V?

6.NS.6

6. Write an algebraic expression for the phrase "*subtract 8 from a*".

xxxxx

DAY 5 ASSESSMENT

1. What is the value of the expression below when $m = 5$ and $n = -6.8$?

$7n - m$

6.EE.2

2. What is the value of the expression below when $u = 0.3$ and $v = 2$?

$15u - v^4 + 31$

6.EE.2

3. Rewrite $6x(5y - z)$ so it is expanded.

6.EE.3

4. Use the Distributive Property to rewrite $16c - 24d$.

6.EE.3

5. What is another way to write $1.9x - 7 + 12.8y + 12.8x - 1 + y$?

6.EE.3

6. Write an expression that is equivalent to $8m + 4(n - 7) - m$.

6.EE.3

DAY 6
CHALLENGE
QUESTION

What expression is twice $8x - 11.5y + 13$?

6.EE.3

Sometimes you need to say something a little differently, the same is true for math! Week 7 gives you practice rewriting numbers and algebraic expressions in different ways so they can be useful for different situations.

You can find detailed video explanations to each problem in the book by visiting:
ArgoPrep.com

DAY 1

To find the surface area of a cube, use the formula
$SA = 6s^2$

---

1. Rewrite the following expression: $a + a + a + a + a - a$.

6.EE.3

---

2. If a cube has side lengths of $\frac{4}{5}$ cm, what is the volume of the cube?

6.EE.2

---

3. What is the surface area of a cube that has side lengths of 5 meters?

6.EE.2

---

4. If a cube has side lengths of $\frac{1}{4}$ foot, what is the volume of the cube?

6.EE.2

---

5. What is the surface area of a cube that has side lengths of 11 mm?

6.EE.2

---

6. What is the least common multiple of 7 and 11?

6.NS.4

The volume of a cube can be found by using the formula $V = s^3$.

DAY 2

1. If a cube has side lengths of *6h* units, what is the volume of the cube?

6.EE.2

2. Rewrite the following expression: *p + q + q + q + p*.

6.EE.3

3. Write an expression that is equivalent to *8g* + 16.

6.EE.3

The coordinates of the vertices of a rectangle are A (3, 1), B (-4, 1), C (-4, -3) and D (3, -3).
Use this information to answer questions 4 – 5.

4. What are the dimensions of the rectangle?

6.NS.8

5. What is the length of Line Segment BC?

6.NS.8

6. What is the value of the expression below?

$5 + 9^2 \times 3$

6.EE.1

DAY 3

Two expressions are equivalent if when a number is substituted in for a variable, the two expressions have the same result.

---

1. What is the surface area of a cube that has side lengths of 5.5 inches?

6.EE.2

---

2. Write an expressions that is equivalent to $5(x + 20)$.

6.EE.4

---

3. If a cube has side lengths of $\frac{3}{4}$ yard, what is the volume of the cube?

6.EE.2

---

4. Write an algebraic expression that is equivalent to: $11b \times 11b \times 11b \times 11b$. Do not evaluate the expression.

6.EE.4

---

5. Write an expression that is equivalent to $3a(5b - 11)$.

6.EE.3

---

6. What is the greatest common factor of 39 and 78?

6.NS.4

1. If a cube has side lengths of $\frac{1}{3}$ foot, what is the volume of the cube?

6.EE.2

2. Write an expression that is equivalent to $w + w + w - w + w$.

6.EE.4

3. What is the surface area of a cube that has side lengths of $10r$ cm?

6.EE.2

4. Write an expression that is equivalent to $c \cdot c \cdot c$.

6.EE.4

5. If a cube has side lengths of $5w$ units, what is the volume of the cube?

6.EE.2

6. What is the value of the expression below when $a = 7.5$ and $b = -3$

$2a - 6b + 2$

6.EE.2

DAY 5 ASSESSMENT

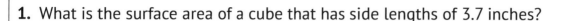

1. What is the surface area of a cube that has side lengths of 3.7 inches?

6.EE.2

2. Write an expression that is equivalent to $6(3z - 2)$.

6.EE.4

3. If a cube has side lengths of $4e$ units, what is the volume of the cube?

6.EE.2

4. Write *"five less than d"* using algebraic terms.

6.EE.2

5. What is the value of n in the equation below?

$0 = -8.09 + n$

6.NS.5

6. In which quadrant would $(5, 7)$ be located?

6.NS.6

DAY 6
CHALLENGE QUESTION

Use the Distributive Property to find an expression that is equivalent to $6(s - 7) - 5(4 - t)$.

6.EE.3

48

WEEK 8

For Week 8 you are given some numbers and you will have a chance to find out which ones are solutions, to make an equation (or inequality) true.

You can find detailed video explanations to each problem in the book by visiting: ArgoPrep.com

DAY 1

1. The set of numbers 0, 1, 3 and 4 contains values for x. What value of x makes the equation below true?

$3x - 9 = 3$

6.EE.5

2. The set of numbers 0, 1, 3 and 4 contains values for y. What value of y makes the equation below true?

$4y - 1 = 11$

6.EE.5

3. The set of numbers 0, 1, 3 and 4 contains values for a. What value of a makes the equation below true?

$10a = 10$

6.EE.5

4. What is the smallest integer value for n that would make $n + 7 > 14$ true?

6.EE.5

5. Write an expression that is equivalent to $3(x + 1)$.

6.EE.4

6. Using the formula $F = 1.8C + 32$, what is the temperature in degrees Fahrenheit when it is $24°C$?

6.EE.2

To determine if a value is a solution to an equation, substitute in the value and see if the number makes the equation true.

DAY 2

---

1. What is the solution to $5b = 25$?

6.EE.7

---

2. What is the largest integer value for x that would make $x + 12 < -1$ true?

6.EE.5

---

3. The set of numbers -1, 3, 8 and 15 contains values for v. What value of v makes the equation below true?

$$\frac{v}{4} + 1 = 3$$

6.EE.5

---

4. What is the solution to $r - 8 = 11$?

6.EE.7

---

5. Write an expression that is equivalent to t^4.

6.EE.4

---

6. What is the value of the expression below if $k = -12$?

$36 - k$

6.EE.2

DAY 3

When looking for solutions to inequalities, often the inequality has more than 1 possible answer that makes the inequality true.

The set of z is shown below. **Use its elements to find the solutions for the equations in questions 1 – 3.**

$z = \{-5, 3, 4, 15\}$

---

1. Which element of z is the solution to: $4z = -20$?

6.EE.5

---

2. Which element of z is the solution to: $20 - z = 5$?

6.EE.5

---

3. Which element of z is the solution to: $5z - 2 = 13$?

6.EE.5

The set of m is shown below. **Use its elements to find the solutions for the equations in questions 4 – 5.**

$m = \{-2, 2, 3, -1, 0\}$

---

4. Which element/s of m is/are the solution/s to: $5m + 3 \geq 3$?

6.EE.5

---

5. Which element/s of m is/are the solution/s to: $-m < 0$?

6.EE.5

---

6. What is $5{,}751 \div 27$?

6.NS.2

TIP of the DAY

Remember when a negative number is being subtracted, it is the same result as if a positive number were being added. For example, 7 − (−2) = 7 + 2.

DAY 4

1. The set of numbers 0, 8, 12 and 15 contains values for q. What value of q makes the equation below true?

$$\frac{q}{4} + 1 = 4$$

6.EE.5

2. What is the solution to $6d = 72$?

6.EE.7

3. What is the solution to $3k = 1$?

6.EE.7

4. What is the largest integer value for b that would make $4b − 5 < −1$ true?

6.EE.5

5. Dylan bought 7 watermelons. If w represents the cost for 1 watermelon, write an expression that could show the cost of 7 watermelons.

6.EE.6

6. Each package of beef is $5.19. If Deb bought b packages of beef, write an expression to represent the cost of all of the beef she bought.

6.EE.6

DAY 5 ASSESSMENT

1. The set of numbers – 4, 0, 5 and 13 contains values for *j*. What value of *j* makes the equation below true?

$2j - 6 = 20$

6.EE.5

2. The set of numbers 5, 8, 10 and 11 contains values for *y*. What value of *y* makes the equation below true?

$3y + 2 = 26$

6.EE.5

3. Write an expression that is equivalent to 7 (3*a*).

6.EE.4

4. What is the smallest integer value for *q* that would make – $3q \leq -11$ true?

6.EE.5

5. What is the solution to $j - 7 = 0$?

6.EE.7

6. Write a true inequality that compares 14.5 and |–15|

6.NS.7

DAY 6
CHALLENGE
QUESTION

Cyrus is *C* years old. If his sister is 8 years older than Cyrus, how old is his sister?

6.EE.2

54

This week you can practice writing your own algebraic expressions by comparing one quantity to another to form a relationship equation.

You can find detailed video explanations to each problem in the book by visiting:
ArgoPrep.com

 **DAY 1**

It is important to choose a variable that will have some meaning. For example, if you are trying to find the number of birds, you may wish to choose b to represent that number.

 TIP of the DAY

1. What is the largest integer value for g that would make $8 - g \geq -8$ true?

6.EE.5

2. Write an expression that is equivalent to $g + g + g + g + g$.

6.EE.4

3. What is the solution to $14s = 7$?

6.EE.7

Dale is d years old. **Use this information to answer questions 4 – 6.**

4. Evan is 3 years older than Dale. How old is Evan?

6.EE.6

5. Ellis is 2 times as old as Dale. How old is Ellis?

6.EE.6

6. Dex is 1 year younger than Dale. How old is Dex?

6.EE.6

1. Elisha put *g* gallons of gas in his car. If the car holds 18 gallons to begin, which expression tells how much gas was in the car before Elisha bought gas?

6.EE.6

2. Emma ran *m* miles, which was $\frac{1}{2}$ as far as Fred ran. How far did Fred run?

6.EE.6

3. Eric wrote *p* pages. Fran wrote 5 pages more than Eric. How many pages did Fran write?

6.EE.6

4. Write an expression that is equivalent to $6p + 5p$.

6.EE.4

5. Dillon's bike is four times as long as his scooter. If his bike is *b*, what is the length of Dillon's scooter?

6.EE.6

6. What is the surface area of a cube that has side lengths of 8 feet?

6.EE.2

 **DAY 3**

A variable can have different values but only one value at a time. For example, x = 4 in x + 3 = 7 but x = -2 in 5x = -10.

The avocados cost *a* dollars. **Use this information to answer questions 1 – 3.**

1. The beans cost 4 dollars less than the avocados. How much did the beans cost?

6.EE.6

2. The plums cost 3 times as much as the avocados. How much did the plums cost?

6.EE.6

3. The kiwi cost one-fourth as much as the avocados. How much did the kiwi cost?

6.EE.6

The coordinates of the vertices of a rectangle are A (-7, 2), B (-7, -1), C (2, -1) and D (2, 2). **Use this information to answer questions 4 – 5.**

4. What are the dimensions of the rectangle?

6.NS.8

5. What is the length of Line Segment AD?

6.NS.8

6. What is the least common multiple of 3 and 9?

6.NS.4

---

1. What is the solution to $6u = 2$?

6.EE.7

---

2. Conrad ate g grapes today, which is 15 more grapes than he ate yesterday. How many grapes did Conrad eat yesterday?

6.EE.6

---

3. The length of the window is w feet, which is 6 times the width. What is the width of the window?

6.EE.6

---

4. The length of the car is 4 feet longer than the motorcycle. If the motorcycle is m feet long, how long is the car?

6.EE.6

---

5. The door is $\frac{1}{3}$ as wide as it is long. If the door is d feet long, how wide is the door?

6.EE.6

---

6. Cherie made n necklaces and Charlotte made four times as many necklaces as Cherie. How many necklaces did Charlotte make?

6.EE.6

 # DAY 5 ASSESSMENT

Donna is *d* inches tall. **Use this information to answer questions 1 – 2.**

1. Faith is $\frac{1}{2}$ as tall as Donna. How tall is Faith?

6.EE.6

2. Gunnar is 3 inches taller than Faith. How tall is Gunnar?

6.EE.6

3. Her first book had *p* pages. Her second book had 12 less pages than her first book. How many pages did her second book have?

6.EE.6

4. Eddy swam his race in *m* minutes. Finn swam the same race but it took him 1 minute longer. How long did it take Finn to swim his race?

6.EE.6

5. What is another way to write *"the quotient of 5 and t"*?

6.EE.2

6. If a cube has side lengths of 8*n* units, what is the volume of the cube?

6.EE.2

 **DAY 6**
CHALLENGE QUESTION

There is a square that has an area that is $121x^2$ square centimeters. What is the length of the square and what is the perimeter of the square?

6.EE.2

WEEK 10

ARGOPREP.COM

VIDEO EXPLANATIONS

In Week 10 you have an opportunity to write your own equations or inequalities to make them fit any situation you are given. Inequalities allow you the chance to have answers that include more than one number.

You can find detailed video explanations to each problem in the book by visiting:
ArgoPrep.com

Chuck spent $27 to buy 5 toys. *T* represents one toy. **Use this information to answer questions 1 – 2.**

1. Write an equation that could be used to find the number of toys Chuck bought.

6.EE.7

2. What was the cost for one toy?

6.EE.7

Fidelo purchased 9 hats for $70.74. Use *h* to represent one hat.
Use this information to answer questions 3 – 4.

3. Write an equation that could be used to find the cost of a one hat.

6.EE.7

4. What was the cost for one hat?

6.EE.7

5. What is the solution to this equation: $8w = 17.6$?

6.EE.7

6. Express *"y less than 7"* as an algebraic expression.

6.EE.2

Gracie walked *m* miles at the zoo. **Use this information to answer questions 1 – 4.**

1. Glen walked 9 miles less than Gracie. How far did Glen walk?

6.EE.6

2. If Gracie walked 12 miles, how far did Glen walk?

6.EE.7

3. Together Hope and Gracie walked 16 miles. How far did Hope walk?

6.EE.6

4. Gracie walked 2 miles less than Harrison. How far did Harrison walk?

6.EE.6

5. What is the solution to this equation: $v + 3.6 = 9$?

6.EE.7

6. Brent's weight was no more than 105 pounds. Write an inequality that shows how many pounds, *b*, Brent weighed.

6.EE.8

DAY 3

---

1. What is the solution to this equation: $\frac{1}{5}l = 5$?

6.EE.7

---

2. The fish tank can only hold 34 fish. There are already 22 fish in the tank. How many more fish, f, can the tank hold? Write an inequality to answer this question.

6.EE.8

---

3. To pass the class, Grant must score at least an 93 on his next exam. If his next exam is e, write an inequality that shows the score Grant will need to pass.

6.EE.8

---

4. What is n on the number line below?

6.EE.8

---

5. What is the solution to this equation: $c + 25.1 = 40$?

6.EE.7

---

6. George drove for more than 20 hours last week. Write an inequality to show how many hours, h, George drove.

6.EE.8

TIP of the **DAY** *When showing an inequality on a number line, if the dot is NOT colored in, or is just a circle, then that point is NOT a part of the solution.*

DAY 4

1. There are 48 turtles at the turtle sanctuary. They are kept in 3 different areas. Write an equation that can be used to find the number of turtles, *t*, in one area?

6.EE.7

2. There are 60 students in 4 classes. Write an equation that can be used to find the number of students, *s*, in one class.

6.EE.7

3. To get a medal, Iris must score more than 9.35 on the vault. Write an inequality to show the score, *s*, Iris must get to earn a medal.

6.EE.8

4. To get a scholarship, Henry can get no more than 18 wrong on the exam. If his exam is *e*, write an inequality that could show the number Henry can get wrong and still earn a scholarship.

6.EE.8

5. What is *n* on the number line below?

6.NS.8

6. Express "*4 less than 8 times t*" as an algebraic expression.

6.EE.2

DAY 5 ASSESSMENT

---

1. Jamie hiked at least 9 hours yesterday. Write an inequality that shows how many hours, *h*, Jamie hiked.

6.EE.8

---

2. In order to ride the kiddie cars a rider cannot weigh more than 50 pounds. Write an inequality to show the weight, *w*, of a kiddie car rider.

6.EE.8

---

3. What is the largest integer value for *n* that would make $n + 2 \leq 15$ true?

6.EE.5

---

4. The tissue box originally held 150 tissues. Gena was sick and used 73 tissues. How many tissues remain?

6.EE.7

---

5. What is the solution for $\frac{2}{3} k = 12$?

6.EE.7

---

6. Henley has 4 times as many socks as he needs. If he has 96 socks, write an equation that could be used to find *s*, the number of socks he needs.

6.EE.7

DAY 6
CHALLENGE QUESTION

Write the inequality for *z* that is shown below.   *6.EE.8*

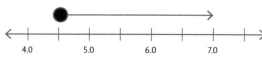

WEEK 11

ARGOPREP.COM

VIDEO EXPLANATIONS

In Week 11 you will practice using 2 variables that change in relation to each other. These are called dependent variables and have a consistent relationship with one another. You will also explore ratios.

You can find detailed video explanations to each problem in the book by visiting:
ArgoPrep.com

 **DAY I** *Two quantities that change in relation to each other have a relationship with one another.*

1. Write an equation to show the relationship of the data.

x	y
4	1
12	3
8	2

6.EE.9

2. Jamal bought 5 pairs of shoes for $126. Write an equation to show the relationship between the number of shoes, *s*, and *C*, the total cost for the shoes.

6.EE.9

3. Tires are priced at $95 each. Write an equation to show the relationship between *C*, the cost of the tires and *t*, the number of tires.

6.EE.9

The graph below shows the sticks of butter, *b*, (horizontal axis) that are needed for every cup of sugar, *s* (on the vertical axis). **Use the information shown below to answer questions 4 – 5.**

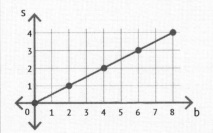

4. Write an equation that shows the relationship between butter and sugar as seen in the graph.

6.EE.9

5. How many cups of sugar are needed for 4 sticks of butter?

6.EE.9

TIP of the DAY

If you have an equation, as long as you have one of the numbers, you can substitute it into the equation to find the missing number.

DAY 2

1. The speed limit, s, has a minimum speed you can travel on an expressway without receiving a ticket. If the minimum speed limit is 45 miles per hour (mph), write an inequality to show the minimum speed. (It is understood that the speed will also be less than the maximum speed limit.)

6.EE.8

2. Jayson drove his RV 350 miles, m, on 25 gallons of gas, g. Write an equation to show the relationship between the number of miles driven and the gallons of gas.

6.EE.9

3. Write an equation that represents the data from the chart.

x	y
2	3
4	6
5	7.5

6.EE.9

4. Which value(s) of Set G are true for the equation $3g > 6.5$?

$\{-3, -2, 1, 4, 5\}$

6.EE.5

5. Ira slept $5\frac{1}{2}$ hours longer than Jessica. If Ira slept h hours, how many hours did Jessica sleep?

6.EE.6

 **DAY 3**

In ratios, the order matters. 12:5 is not the same as 5:12.

Below are the number of people who attended a ball game. **Use this table below to answer questions 1 – 5.**

Adults (ages 12 – 54 years)	24
Youth (ages 2 – 10 years)	44
Seniors (ages over 55 years)	16
Babies (ages under 2 years)	2

1. What is the ratio of youth to adults?

6.RP.1

2. What is the ratio of seniors to adults?

6.RP.1

3. What is the ratio of seniors to babies?

6.RP.1

4. What is the ratio of youth to babies?

6.RP.1

5. What is the ratio of babies to all those who attended the game?

6.RP.1

Below are the number of times 4 books at the library were checked out. **Use this table below to answer questions 1 – 4.**

A Wrinkle in Time	27
Tarzan	18
Winnie the Pooh	12
Nancy Drew #47	33

1. What is the ratio of times Tarzan was checked out compared to Nancy Drew #47?

6.RP.1

2. What is the ratio of times the Winnie the Pooh was checked out compared to A Wrinkle in Time?

6.RP.1

3. What is the ratio of times Nancy Drew #47 was checked out compared to Winnie the Pooh?

6.RP.1

4. What is the ratio of times A Wrinkle in Time was checked out compared to the other books?

6.RP.1

5. Jenna ran 3 times as fast as James. If Jenna had a speed of *J*, what was James' speed?

6.EE.6

1. There were 12 orange ribbons for every 4 purple ribbons. What is the ratio of purple ribbons to orange ribbons?

6.RP.1

2. Write an equation to represent the data shown below.

x	y
5	4
2.5	2
7.5	6

6.EE.9

3. Each pound of potatoes is $1.15. Write an equation that could be used to find the cost, C, of p pounds of potatoes.

6.EE.9

4. The ratio of plums to nectarines is 2:3. If there are 6 plums, how many nectarines are there?

6.RP.1

5. Write an equation to represent the data shown below.

x	y
1	2
3	6
2.5	5

6.EE.9

 **DAY 6** CHALLENGE QUESTION

Using the table from #5, if x = 7.5, what would be the value of y?

6.EE.9

During Week 12, you will further your knowledge of ratios by studying unit rates to solve real-world problems using tables and percents.

You can find detailed video explanations to each problem in the book by visiting:
ArgoPrep.com

 **DAY 1**

The unit rate is the amount of money (or time or something else) per ONE thing. Miles per hour is a unit rate because it tells the number of miles a person travels in ONE hour.

 TIP of the DAY

---

1. If Jasmine spent $280 on 20 pairs of earrings, what was the cost of 1 pair?

6.RP.2

---

2. If 20 cookies use 16 ounces of nuts, how many ounces of nuts are in 1 cookie?

6.RP.2

---

3. An 18 ounce bottle of juice costs $4.86. What is the unit rate for the juice?

6.RP.2

---

4. A 20-ounce container of shampoo was $2.60. How much was 1 ounce of shampoo? Round your answer to the nearest cent.

6.RP.2

---

5. Levi works 8 hours each day of work. He works every day for 10 days. If he made $620 during those 10 days, how much does Levi make per hour?

6.RP.2

---

6. Ezra uses 24 teaspoons of vanilla for 192 cups of cream cheese for his cheesecakes. If he only had 1 cup of cream cheese, how many teaspoons of vanilla would he use?

6.RP.2

When comparing prices of 2 items, it is better to find the unit rate of each package rather than just looking at the overall cost of a package.

DAY 2

1. Jeff is taking a biology class. He studies 4 hours each day. If his grade improved by 6 points over 3 days of studying, how many points does his grade improve per hour studied?

6.RP.2

2. The sprinklers run 5 hours each day. The monthly (30 days) water bill is $500. How much does it cost to run the sprinklers for an hour? Round your answer to the nearest cent.

6.RP.2

3. Jake purchased 6 packages of burgers for $53.76. Each package contains 8 burgers. How much did Jake pay for 1 burger?

6.RP.2

4. Olive oil is $7.98 for 36 ounces. What is its unit rate? Round your answer to the nearest cent.

6.RP.2

5. Brinks uses 2 gallons of gas per lawn mowed. He mows 5 lawns per day for 10 days. If he had to pay $249 for gas during those 10 days, how much would he pay for 1 gallon of gas?

6.RP.2

6. The maximum weight for the elevator was 500 pounds. Write an inequality that shows the weight, *w*, it can hold.

6.EE.8

1. Fiber-Brite could clean 48 rugs in 12 hours. At that rate, how many rugs could Fiber-Brite clean in 20 hours?

6.RP.3

Below is a table showing the cost and sizes of some meats and cheeses from the deli. **Use this information to answer questions 2 – 5.**

Product	Ounces	Price
Mozzarella cheese	32	$15.98
Roast beef	9	$6.75
Muenster cheese	16	$7.29
Turkey	18	$11.49

2. Which food has the lowest per ounce cost?

6.RP.3

3. Which food has the highest per ounce cost?

6.RP.3

4. Which 2 foods are closest in price per ounce?

6.RP.3

5. How much would you expect 16 ounces of roast beef to cost?

6.RP.3

TIP of the **DAY**

Below is a table showing 4 employees and how many dollars they earned while working (in hours). **Use this information to answer questions 1 – 3.** If necessary, round your answers to the nearest cent.

Employee	Pay	Time (hours)
Irma	$40	3.5
Jaxon	$85	10
Kelsey	$17	1.5
Lara	$58	6

1. Which employee makes the most per hour?

6.RP.3

2. Which employee has the lowest hourly rate?

6.RP.3

3. How much would Kelsey make in 24 minutes?

6.RP.3

4. Express *"the difference of twelve and x, multiplied by y"* as an algebraic expression.

6.EE.2

5. What is the solution to this equation: $6r = 33$?

6.EE.7

Justin bought 7 1/2 dozen candy bars for $51. **Use this information to answer questions 1 – 2.** If needed, round your answers to the nearest cent.

1. How much did Justin pay per dozen?

6.RP.2

2. If Justin bought 18 candy bars, how much would it cost?

6.RP.3

3. A pizza contains 8 slices of pizza. A pizza costs $12.80 except on Tuesday when it is $0.25 off per slice. What is the cost of 1 slice of pizza on Tuesdays?

6.RP.3

4. The morning bus route is 18 miles long and takes 40 minutes. The afternoon route takes 54 minutes (and is the same distance). How much longer does it take to travel a mile during the afternoon route? Round your answer to the nearest hundredth of a minute.

6.RP.3

5. Write an equation that represents the data in the chart below.

x	y
2	6
2.5	7.5
3	9

6.EE.9

DAY 6
CHALLENGE
QUESTION

Keeley drove 513 miles in 9 hours on Tuesday. On Wednesday she increased her speed by 2 mph. If she travels at this new speed for 7 hours, how far will she travel?

6.RP.3

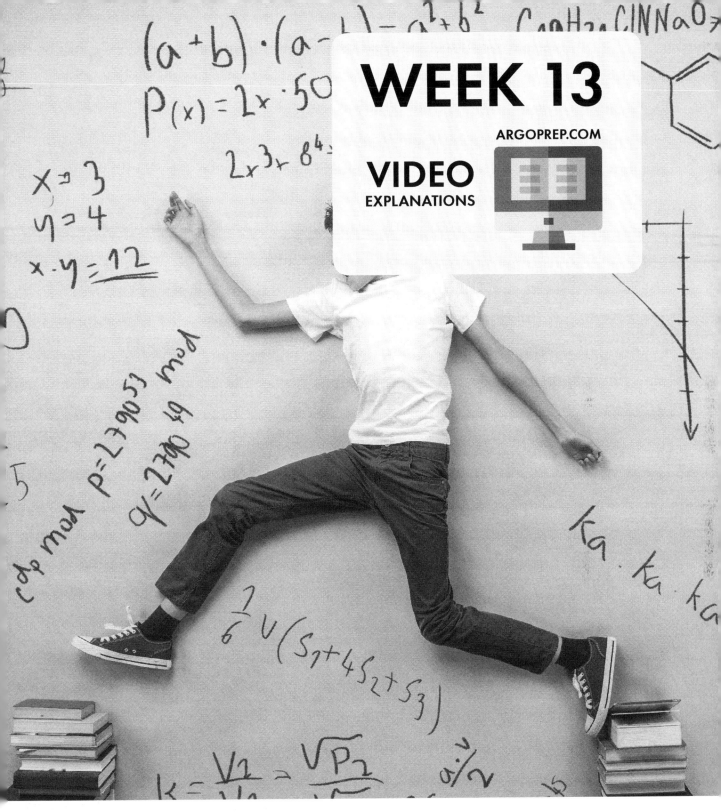

Got questions? If you do, then Week 13 is the right place for you! It is all about statistical questions and identifying what would be good questions to ask when looking for specific data.

You can find detailed video explanations to each problem in the book by visiting:
ArgoPrep.com

 **DAY 1**

Usually the word "OF" in a math problem indicates multiplication.

If appropriate, round your answer to the nearest tenth or tenth of a percent.

1. What is 23% of 400?

6.RP.3

2. 25 is what percent of 150?

6.RP.3

3. What is 150% of 72?

6.RP.3

4. 70 is what percent of 50?

6.RP.3

5. The coordinates of the vertices of a rectangle are A (3, 5), B (3, -1), C (-2, -1) and D (-2, 5). What are the dimensions of the rectangle?

6.NS.8

6. How many cups of sugar could be placed in 4 bowls if $\frac{7}{8}$ cup of sugar is split evenly among those bowls?

6.NS.1

If appropriate, round your answer to the nearest tenth or tenth of a percent.

1. What is 32% of 88?

6.RP.3

2. What is 300% of 12?

6.RP.3

3. 61 is what percent of 183?

6.RP.3

4. 21 is 25% of what number?

6.RP.3

5. How many fifths are in $3\frac{1}{10}$?

6.NS.1

6. What is 3,276 ÷ 28?

6.NS.2

 **DAY 3** *A statistical question is one in which there are several possible answers.*

---

1. It took Jodi 8 hours to vacuum 9,600 square feet of offices. At this rate, how long would it take Jodi to vacuum 2,400 square feet?

---

2. Using the table below, what is the missing number?

x	y
1	4.5
2	?
3	13.5

---

3. If there are 120 vests and 30% of them are blue, how many blue vests are there?

---

4. Mary Kay can sell 150 lipsticks in 2 months. How many lipsticks could she sell in 7 months?

---

5. Jolene is $\frac{1}{3}$ as tall as Kevin. If Kevin's height was k, what was Jolene's height?

1. Explain why the question below is NOT a statistical question.

How many pairs of shoes do you own?

6.SP.1

2. Explain why the question below is NOT a statistical question.

Do you like yogurt?

6.SP.1

3. Explain why the question below is NOT a statistical question.

What did Lilith score on the balance beam?

6.SP.1

4. Explain why the question below is NOT a statistical question.

How many burritos did Mark eat?

6.SP.1

5. What is the least common multiple of 6 and 11?

6.NS.4

6. There are 48 animals and 12 of them are cats. What is the ratio of cats to animals?

6.RP.1

DAY 5 ASSESSMENT

1. Lynn hiked for 15 minutes and traveled 2 kilometers. If she kept the same pace, how far would she hike in 2.5 hours?

6.RP.3

2. Using the table below, what is the missing number?

x	y
3	4
?	8
1.5	2

6.RP.3

3. 26 is what percent of 130?

6.RP.3

4. Explain why the question below is NOT a statistical question.

Did it rain today?

6.SP.1

5. What is 0.6% of 500?

6.RP.3

DAY 6 CHALLENGE QUESTION

Write a statistical question.

6.SP.1

WEEK 14

ARGOPREP.COM

VIDEO EXPLANATIONS

This week starts the beginning of a detailed study of data. You will begin to see how numbers in a data set relate to the set as a whole.

You can find detailed video explanations to each problem in the book by visiting:
ArgoPrep.com

DAY 1

The median is the middle number when all the data are in order from smallest to largest.

High temperatures for the week are recorded below. **Use this information to answer questions 1 – 3.** Round your answer to the nearest hundredth.

Test scores:	77	82	79	81	76	78	84

1. What is the median of the data?

6.SP.2

2. What is the range of the data?

6.SP.2

3. What is the mean of the data?

6.SP.2

Below is the number of days 15 students were absent. **Use this information to answer questions 4 – 6.**

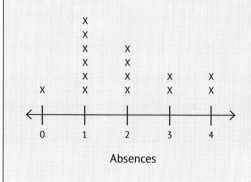

Absences

4. How many days was a student most likely to be absent?

6.SP.2

5. What is the mean of the data? Round your answer to the nearest tenth.

6.SP.2

6. What is the range of the data set?

6.SP.2

Mika was bowling and she recorded how many pins she knocked down on 10 tries. Her data is shown below. **Use the given information to answer questions 1 – 3.**

Try #	Pins	Try #	Pins
1	5	6	6
2	4	7	8
3	7	8	7
4	5	9	9
5	6	10	8

1. What is the range of Mika's data?

6.SP.2

2. What is the median of the data set? Round your answer to the nearest tenth.

6.SP.2

3. What is the mean of the data? Round your answer to the nearest tenth.

6.SP.2

4. You can buy 1 pound of chocolate for $7.99. How much is the chocolate per ounce? Round your answer to the nearest cent.

6.RP.2

5. Write an expression that is equivalent to $25k - 10$.

6.EE.4

DAY 3

The range is the difference between the largest and the smallest numbers in a data set.

Kurt kept track of how much his family spent eating out. His results are below and are given in dollars. **Use the given information to answer questions 1 – 3.**

22	37
45	32
33	31
28	35

1. What is the range of the data set?

6.SP.2

2. What is the median of the data set? Round your answer to the nearest tenth.

6.SP.2

3. What is the mean of the data? Round your answer to the nearest tenth.

6.SP.2

4. What is the value of the expression below?

$7 + 2^5 \times 3$

6.EE.1

5. Kenzi bought 12 belts for $54. Write an equation that shows the relationship between the number of belts, b, and C, the total cost for the belts.

6.EE.9

Mean is another way to say average. It can be found by adding all of a set of numbers together and then dividing by however many numbers were added.

DAY 4

Below shows the number of pages that students read of over the weekend.
Use this information to answer questions 1 – 4.

	Pages			
0	3	5	5	6
1	2	7	8	
2	1	3	3	7
3	0			

---

1. What is the range of the data set?

6.SP.2

---

2. What is the median of the data set? Round your answer to the nearest tenth.

6.SP.2

---

3. What is the mean of the data? Round your answer to the nearest tenth.

6.SP.2

---

4. Which numbers are the modes?

6.SP.2

---

5. The tubing was 146 feet long. If each piece of tubing was cut so that it was 6 feet long, how many 6-foot pieces could be made from the tubing?

6.NS.2

The number of yards that some football players ran is listed below.
Use this information to answer questions 1 – 4.

Yards:	42	17	8	50	11	33	26	19

1. What is the range of the data set?

6.SP.2

2. What is the median of the data set? Round your answer to the nearest tenth.

6.SP.2

3. What is the mean of the data? Round your answer to the nearest tenth.

6.SP.2

4. Which measure of center gives the most accurate picture of the data set?

6.SP.2

5. Write an equation that is represented in the data chart below.

x	y
20	4
5	1
12.5	2.5

6.EE.9

DAY 6
CHALLENGE
QUESTION

Using the data from questions 1 – 4, if the 8 was removed from the data set, what would be the new mean? Round your answer to the nearest tenth. 6.SP.2

WEEK 15

VIDEO EXPLANATIONS

ARGOPREP.COM

You will have plenty of opportunities to find numbers that summarize and help to describe given sets of data. Week 15 focuses on measures of center.

You can find detailed video explanations to each problem in the book by visiting:
ArgoPrep.com

DAY 1

TIP of the DAY

Mr. Scantonelli's class recorded all of their heights and the information is shown below.
Please use the box plot below to answer questions 1 – 3.

Height (in)

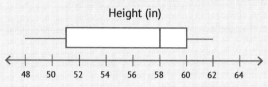

48 50 52 54 56 58 60 62 64

---

1. What is the median of the data set?

6.SP.3

---

2. What is the range of the data set?

6.SP.3

---

3. What is the inter-quartile range (IQR) of the data set?

6.SP.3

---

4. Why is the following NOT a statistical question?

How many points did Johnny score last night?

6.SP.1

---

5. Candace's bank account had a balance of - $394.07. She deposited $100 into the account. What would she need to do to have a zero balance on her account?

6.NS.5

---

6. 45 is what percent of 360?

6.RP.3

Miss Foster's class made paper chains. Each student measured their chain to see how long it was. The results are below. **Use this information to answer questions 1 – 3.**

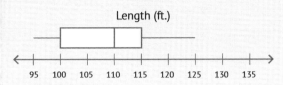

1. What is the inter-quartile range (IQR) for the data set shown?

6.SP.3

2. What is the range for the data set shown?

6.SP.3

3. What is the median of the data set?

6.SP.3

4. What is the value of the expression below?

$8 + 3^4 - (5^2 - 14)$

6.EE.1

5. The coordinates of the vertices of a rectangle are A (-4, 2), B (1, 2), C (1, -6) and D (-4, -6). What is the length of segment BC?

6.NS.8

6. What is the perimeter of the rectangle in #5?

6.NS.8

DAY 3

Range helps determine the amount of variance in a data set.

TIP of the DAY

Leo weighed the pets in the pet store. Their weights (in pounds) are shown below.
Arrange the data into a box plot to answer questions 1 – 4.

Weights:	12	25	7	13	18	9	14

1. What is the range for the data set shown?

6.SP.3

2. What is the median of the data set?

6.SP.3

3. What is the inter-quartile range (IQR) for the data set shown?

6.SP.3

4. What is the mean of the data set?

6.SP.2

5. There are 108 boats and 9 of them are green. What is the ratio of green boats to total boats?

6.RP.1

6. If there are 56 firefighters and 30% of them go home to sleep, how many of the firefighters sleep at home? Round your answer to the nearest whole number.

6.RP.3

TIP of the **DAY** — *When considering box plots, be sure to read the labels on the number line.*

Levi's chemistry scores are shown below. **Use this data to answer questions 1 – 3.**

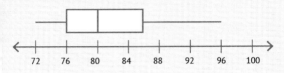

---

1. What is the median of the data set?

6.SP.3

---

2. What is the inter-quartile range (IQR) for the data set shown?

6.SP.3

---

3. What is the range for the data set shown?

6.SP.3

---

4. The area of the pool cover is 1,774 $\frac{1}{2}$ square meters. The width of the cover is 22 $\frac{3}{4}$ meters. What is the length, in meters, of the cover?

6.NS.1

Use the rectangular coordinate system and the parallelogram shown below to answer questions 5 – 6.

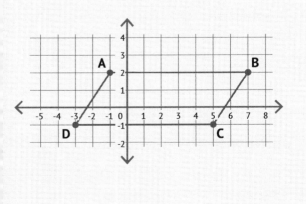

5. What is the distance of Line Segment AB?

6.NS.8

6. What is the distance of Line Segment CD?

6.NS.8

Lydia's English scores are shown below. **Use the given information to answer questions 1 – 3.**

	English Scores				
7	5	7			
8	3	5	8	8	
9	3	4	7	8	9
10	0				

1. What is the range of the data set?

6.SP.3

2. What is the mean for the data set shown (rounded to the tenths)?

6.SP.3

3. What is the median of the data set?

6.SP.3

4. What is the least common multiple of 9 and 8?

6.NS.4

5. 500 is what percent of 450? (Round to the nearest whole percent.)

6.RP.3

6. Lexie can run around the block in 6 minutes and Meghan can run around the block in 8 minutes. If they start running at their house at the same time and run continuously, how many minutes until they will both be back at their house?

6.NS.4

DAY 6
CHALLENGE
QUESTION

Using the data set from #'s 1 – 4 shown above, if all of Lydia's scores are shown, how many assignments did Lydia have in her English class?

6.SP.5

In Week 16 you will have the chance to zoom in on data sets so you can see how each piece of data combines with the other data points to form one large plot that represents the whole data set.

You can find detailed video explanations to each problem in the book by visiting:
ArgoPrep.com

DAY 1

When plotting data, there should be one plot for each piece of data in the set.

TIP of the **DAY**

Use the tables below to answer questions 1 – 4.

Table A

1	4	5
2	1	7
3	8	1
1	3	4
1	2	2

Table B

6	7	4
2	4	1
3	6	2
7	6	3
2	1	7

Table C

2	6	5
3	2	3
1	5	4
5	6	3
4	4	6

Table D

6	4	3
4	2	4
5	3	5
4	6	7
3	6	4

---

1. Which data set is shown below?

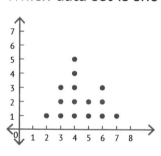

6.SP.4

2. Which data set is shown below?

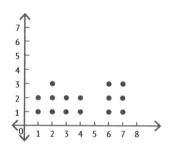

6.SP.4

3. Which data set is shown below?

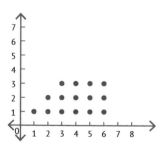

6.SP.4

4. Which data set is shown below?

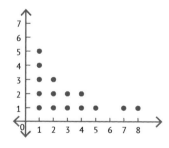

6.SP.4

---

5. Create a dot plot for the data shown below.

5	4	2	3	5
6	7	5	4	6
4	5			

6.SP.4

98

Data can be shown in a variety of ways. Information can be plotted on graphs, dot plots, box plots and other methods.

DAY 2

Use the four plots shown below to answer questions 1 – 4.

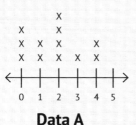

Data A

Data B

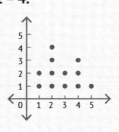

Data C

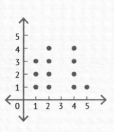

Data D

---

1. Which data graph above shows the data from the set below?

1, 2, 4, 2, 2, 5, 3, 1, 4, 2, 3, 4

6.SP.4

---

2. Which data graph above shows the data from the set below?

0, 3, 4, 5, 2, 3, 1, 3, 5, 2, 5, 4

6.SP.4

---

3. Which data graph above shows the data from the set below?

2, 1, 4, 2, 4, 5, 1, 4, 4, 2, 2, 1

6.SP.4

---

4. Which data graph above shows the data from the set below?

2, 4, 3, 1, 5, 2, 4, 4, 1, 2, 3, 2

6.SP.4

---

5. Using the table below, what is the missing number?

x	y
1.5	?
9	3
6	2

6.RP.3

DAY 3

Histograms are useful to show periods of time or numbers.

Below are 4 histograms that show the number of named storms during 10-year periods of time. **Use the 4 histograms below to answer questions 1 – 4.**

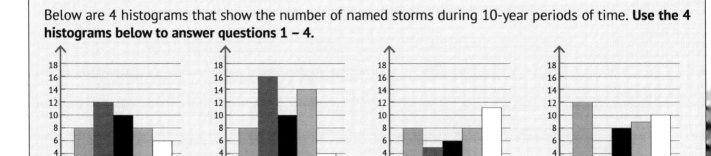

Graph A **Graph B** **Graph C** **Graph D**

---

1. Look at the tally mark chart below, which data set is being graphed?

Time Period	Storms
1970 - 1979	JHT III
1980 - 1989	JHT JHT JHT I
1990 - 1999	JHT JHT
2000 - 2009	JHT JHT IIII
2010 - 2020	IIII

6.SP.4

2. Look at the tally mark chart below, which data set is being graphed?

Time Period	Storms
1970 - 1979	JHT JHT II
1980 - 1989	III
1990 - 1999	JHT III
2000 - 2009	JHT IIII
2010 - 2020	JHT JHT

6.SP.4

3. Look at the tally mark chart below, which data set is being graphed?

Time Period	Storms
1970 - 1979	JHT III
1980 - 1989	JHT JHT II
1990 - 1999	JHT JHT
2000 - 2009	JHT III
2010 - 2020	JHT I

6.SP.4

4. Look at the tally mark chart below, which data set is being graphed?

Time Period	Storms
1970 - 1979	JHT III
1980 - 1989	JHT
1990 - 1999	JHT I
2000 - 2009	JHT III
2010 - 2020	JHT JHT I

6.SP.4

---

5. Britney read 12 books and earned 5 markers. Write an equation to show the relationship between the number of books read, b, and m, the number of markers.

6.EE.9

When graphing data, make sure to count the pieces of data to make sure each piece is present in the graph or plot.

DAY 4

Below are four data tables. **Use the tables below to answer questions 1 – 4**

Table A

1	3	4	6
4	7	2	2
2	4	6	4

Table B

8	2	2	4
4	1	4	6
2	7	2	7

Table C

3	7	6	4
1	2	4	1
2	2	1	6

Table D

8	2	1	2
5	7	6	8
2	3	8	5

---

1. Which data set is graphed below?

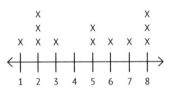

6.SP.4

---

2. Which data set is graphed below?

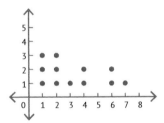

6.SP.4

---

3. Which data set is graphed below?

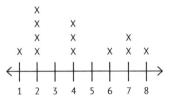

6.SP.4

---

4. Which data set is graphed below?

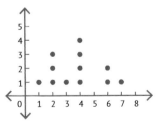

6.SP.4

---

5. Candace made donuts and could package 11 of them in each box. If she made 3,908 donuts, how many full boxes would she have?

6.NS.2

DAY 5 ASSESSMENT

Four different students surveyed 25 strangers about the number of times that they had flown in a plane. The students recorded the information in different ways and the plots of their surveys are shown below. **Use these graphs to answer questions 1 – 4.**

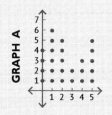
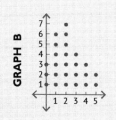
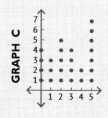
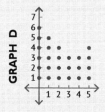

1. Which graph shows the data set below?

Times on Plane	People
0	IIII
1	III
2	IIII
3	IIII
4	II
5	IIII II

6.SP.4

2. Which graph shows the data set below?

Times on Plane	People
0	IIII
1	IIII I
2	IIII
3	II
4	III
5	IIII

6.SP.4

3. Which graph shows the data set below?

Data Set	0	2	1	1	5	2	4	1	3	2	0	2	1	3	4	2	1	0	2	4	5	3	1	2	3

6.SP.4

4. Which graph shows the data set below?

Data Set	0	2	4	0	1	5	0	3	2	0	5	1	0	3	0	1	4	2	5	1	3	2	1	5	4

6.SP.4

5. What is the mean of Graph A from above?

6.SP.3

DAY 6
CHALLENGE QUESTION

1	4	3
3	1	3
2	5	2
4	4	3

Create a dot plot using the following data set. 6.SP.4

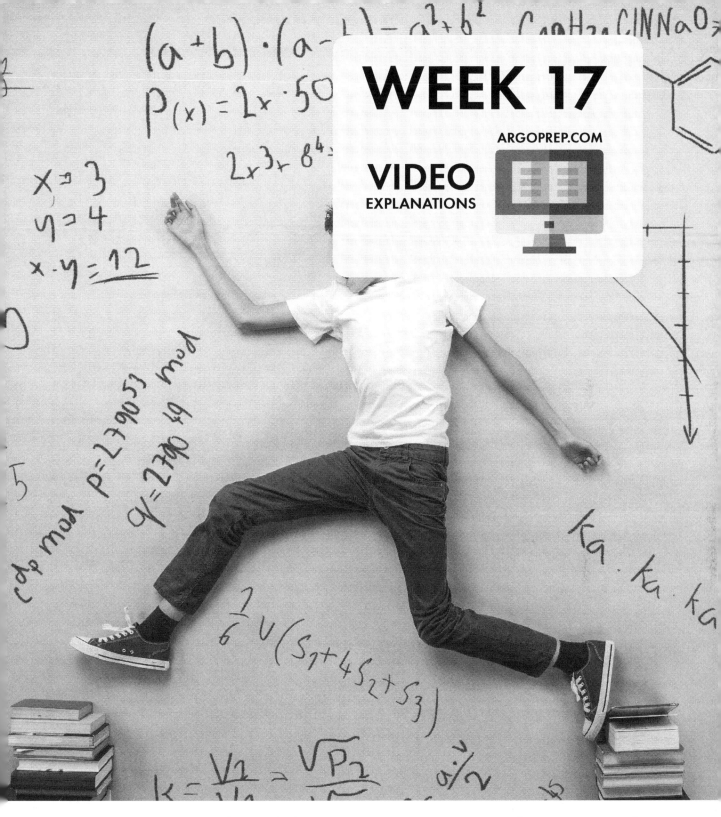

This week you can begin to see what each data piece represents. How many observations were there? How was the data measured? What is the mean or median of the data set?

You can find detailed video explanations to each problem in the book by visiting:
ArgoPrep.com

The chart below shows the number of muffins 4 bakers made. **Use the table below to answer questions 1 – 3.**

Baker	Muffins
Karla	12 dozen
Lena	151
Paula	8 dozen
Daisy	97

1. How many muffins did Karla make?

6.SP.5

2. Which baker made the most muffins?

6.SP.5

3. Which 2 bakers made almost the same number of muffins?

6.SP.5

4. Michelle has 18 more toys than Susan. If Michelle has *M* toys, how many toys does Susan have?

6.EE.6

5. Which value(s) of Set *K* are true for the equation $4k \geq -3$?

$\{-4, -1, 0, 2, 3, 5\}$

6.EE.5

6. What is 0.5% of 42?

6.RP.3

The dot plot below shows how many times each student in Mrs. Carter's class rode the ferris wheel. **Use the information to answer questions 1 – 5.**

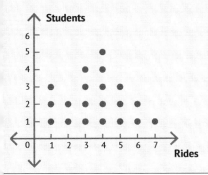

1. What is the largest number of times any one student rode the ferris wheel?

6.SP.5

2. How many times did the most students ride?

6.SP.5

3. How many students are in Mrs. Carter's class?

6.SP.5

4. How many students only rode 1 time?

6.SP.5

5. What is the TOTAL number of times the Ferris wheel was ridden by a student in Mrs. Carter's class?

6.SP.5

6. The width of a sheet is $7\frac{1}{4}$ feet. If the area of the sheet is 87 square feet, what is the length of the sheet?

6.NS.1

DAY 3

You are doing great! You have completed over 16 weeks worth of work – keep it up

Below is a graph showing the favorite colors of 6th graders at Wever Middle School. **Use this information to answer questions 1 – 6.**

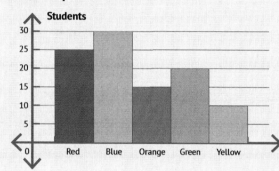

1. Which color do most 6th graders say is their favorite?

6.SP.5

2. How many students were polled about their favorite color?

6.SP.5

3. How many students said orange was their favorite?

6.SP.5

4. How many students said red OR green was their favorite?

6.SP.5

5. What is the ratio of students who have blue as their favorite color to the number of students who have yellow as their favorite color?

6.RP.1

6. What is the ratio of students who have red as their favorite color to the number of students who participated in the survey?

6.RP.1

Each student in Mrs. Shirlen's class was asked how many books they had in their bedroom at home. The results are below. **Use this information to answer questions 1 – 6.**

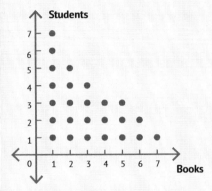

---

1. What is the largest number of books that EVERY student has in their room?

6.SP.5

---

2. What is the largest number of books that any ONE student has?

6.SP.5

---

3. How many students are in Mrs. Shirlen's class?

6.SP.5

---

4. How many books in TOTAL are represented on the graph?

6.SP.5

---

5. What is the mean number of the data?

6.SP.3

---

6. What is the median number of the data?

6.SP.3

DAY 5 ASSESSMENT

Students were asked what their favorite main dish was. Their answers are shown below.
Use this information to answer questions 1 – 6.

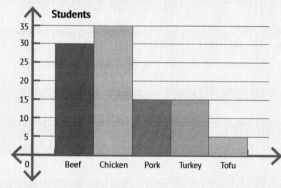

1. Which food did the fewest students say was their favorite?

6.SP.5

2. Which dish did the most students say was their favorite?

6.SP.5

3. Which dish did 30 students vote for?

6.SP.5

4. Which 2 dishes got the same number of votes?

6.SP.5

5. What is the ratio of votes for pork to votes for turkey?

6.RP.1

6. What is the ratio between votes for all meats to votes for chicken?

6.RP.1

DAY 6
CHALLENGE QUESTION

Using the table from above, what is the total number of students who stated their favorite meat? 6.SP.5

If you ever need to buy carpet for a room or plant grass in your backyard, you will need to know how to find the area of the carpet and grass. Week 18 gives you lots of practice finding the area of figures.

You can find detailed video explanations to each problem in the book by visiting:
ArgoPrep.com

DAY 1

When finding the area of a triangle or a trapezoid, remember to divide by 2.

---

1. What is the area of the figure below?

Length: 7.5 cm

Width: 4 cm

6.G.1

---

2. The octagon below is made of 8 triangles that each have a base of 5 cm and a height of 4 cm. What is the area of the octagon?

6.G.1

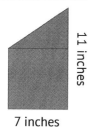

11 inches

7 inches

3. The trapezoid below has been sectioned into a square and a triangle. What is its area?

6.G.1

---

4. What is the area of the shape below?

7.1 m

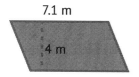

4 m

6.G.1

---

5. The washing machine used 2,860 units of electricity over 11 days. There were 2 loads of laundry run each day. How much energy was used per load?

6.RP.2

---

6. What is the greatest common factor of 56 and 96?

6.NS.4

1. What is the area of the figure below?

5.5 in

12.4 in

6.G.1

2. What is the area of the figure below?

13 inches

13 inches

6.G.1

3. What is the area of the figure below?

4 feet

6.5 feet

7.5 feet

6.G.1

4. What is the area of the figure below?

12.6 in

2 in

6 in

7.5 in

6.G.1

5. Write an equation that represents the data from the chart below.

x	y
1.75	3.5
2.25	4.5
3.75	7.5

6.EE.9

6. What is the area of the figure below?

6 centimeters

46 centimeters

6.G.1

When finding the area of a square, you need to multiply the side lengths, so the formula for the area of a square is $A = s^2$.

TIP of the **DAY**

Use the composite figure below to answer questions 1 – 5. It was measured in centimeters.

4.5 cm | 2 cm

8 cm

10 cm

---

1. What is the area of the square?

6.G.1

---

2. What is the area of the longest (vertical) rectangle?

6.G.1

---

3. What is the area of the shortest (horizontal) rectangle?

6.G.1

---

4. What is the area of the triangle?

6.G.1

---

5. What is the area of the entire figure combined?

6.G.1

---

6. Which value(s) of Set X are true for the equation $5.1X \leq 12$?

{-3, 0, 1, 3, 5}

6.EE.5

---

1. What is the area of the shape below?

11 inches   7 inches   10 inches

6.G.1

2. A square has a side length of 5.5 yards. What is the area of the square?

6.G.1

3. What is the area of the figure below?

9 inches

12 inches

6.G.1

4. What is the area of the figure below?

$\frac{4}{7}$ m

$\frac{2}{5}$ m

6.G.1

5. What is the least common multiple of 7 and 8?

6.NS.4

6. In order to have a healthy heart it is recommended that your "good" cholesterol be more than 100. Write an inequality to show the "healthy" amount of good cholesterol, c.

6.EE.8

The shape below contains a square, a right triangle and 2 rectangles. **Use the information given to answer questions 1 – 4.**

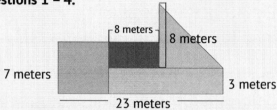

8 meters
8 meters
7 meters
3 meters
23 meters

1. What is the area of the triangle?

6.G.1

2. What is the area of the larger rectangle?

6.G.1

3. What is the total area for the entire figure?

6.G.1

4. What is the area of the hexagon shown that has 6 equilateral triangles?

4.5 mm
12 mm

6.G.1

5. What is the solution to this equation: $d + 3\frac{1}{4} = 17\frac{1}{2}$?

6.EE.7

6. What is the largest integer value for m that would make $-m > 9$ true?

6.EE.5

DAY 6
CHALLENGE
QUESTION

Look at the figure used for #4 above. If the hexagon were changed to a decagon (10-sided) but kept the same area, what would be the are of ONE of its triangles?

6.G.1

ARGOPREP.COM

VIDEO
EXPLANATIONS

In Week 19 you will be able to calculate the volume of three-dimensional objects — or determine the amount of space that that object occupies.

You can find detailed video explanations to each problem in the book by visiting:
ArgoPrep.com

 **DAY I**

Three dimensions are needed to find volume (length x width x height).

1. What is the volume of a rectangular prism that is $6\frac{1}{2}$ inches tall, 5 inches wide and $9\frac{1}{4}$ inches deep? Round to the nearest tenth.

6.G.2

2. The rectangular prism below is made of cubes that have $\frac{1}{4}$ - centimeter sides. What is the volume of the prism? Round to the nearest tenth.

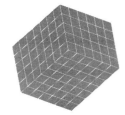

6.G.2

3. A right triangular prism has a triangle that is 8.4 cm tall and a base of 11 cm. The depth of the prism is 9.7 cm. What is the volume of this prism?

6.G.2

4. What is the volume of the rectangular prism below?

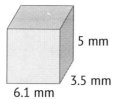

5 mm

3.5 mm

6.1 mm

6.G.2

5. How many quarts of milk would 2 recipes have available if there was $\frac{3}{4}$ - quart of milk to share?

6.NS.1

6. What is 3.9% of 1450?

6.RP.3

1. There is a right triangular prism that has a triangular base. The triangle has a base that is $12\frac{1}{2}$ meters with an 8 meter height. The prism is $15\frac{1}{4}$ meters long. What is the volume of this triangular prism? Round to tenths.

6.G.2

The rectangular prism below is made up of unit squares. **Use this information to answer questions 2 – 3.**

2. If each unit square is 1 m³, what is the volume of the prism?

6.G.2

3. If the above figure's unit cubes had sides that were $\frac{1}{2}$ inch, then what would be the volume of the prism?

6.G.2

4. The figure below has a base that is $\frac{1}{3}$ - centimeter by $\frac{1}{3}$ - centimeter. What is the volume of the figure?

12 centimeters

6.G.2

5. The coordinates of the vertices of a rectangle are A (-1, 3), B (6, 3), C (6, -2) and D (-1, -2). What are the dimensions of the rectangle?

6.NS.8

6. What is 8664 ÷ 76?

6.NS.2

DAY 3

Volume = length x width x height.

---

1. The rectangular prism below is made of cubes that have $\frac{3}{4}$-yard sides. What is the volume of the prism?

6.G.2

---

2. A rectangular prism has a base that is 8 inches wide and is $12\frac{1}{2}$ inches long. If the height is $10\frac{1}{4}$ inches, what is the prism's volume?

6.G.2

---

3. What is the volume of the tent below?

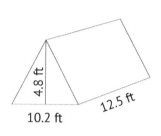

4.8 ft
10.2 ft
12.5 ft

6.G.2

---

4. The rectangular prism below is made of cubes that have $\frac{1}{3}$-inch sides. What is the volume of the prism?

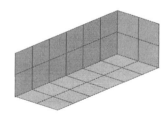

6.G.2

---

5. What is the volume of the rectangular prism below?

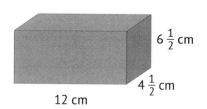

$6\frac{1}{2}$ cm
$4\frac{1}{2}$ cm
12 cm

6.G.2

---

6. What is the range of the data shown below?

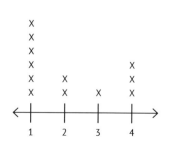

6.SP.3

---

1. What is the volume of the cube below? Round to tenths.

$8\frac{1}{5}$ meters

6.G.2

---

2. There is a prism that is $9\frac{3}{4}$ cm tall. What is its volume if it is a right triangular prism that has a triangle with a base of $8\frac{2}{5}$ cm and a height of 20 cm?

6.G.2

Below are some athletes and the sports they play. **Use the information below to answer questions 3 – 5.**

Football	42
Baseball	48
Soccer	36
Basketball	56

---

3. What is the ratio of basketball to soccer athletes?

6.RP.1

---

4. What is the ratio of football to baseball athletes?

6.RP.1

---

5. What is the ratio of baseball to soccer athletes?

6.RP.1

DAY 5 ASSESSMENT

1. What is the volume of the rectangular prism below? Round your answer to the nearest tenth.

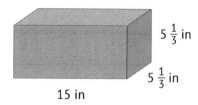

$5\frac{1}{3}$ in

$5\frac{1}{3}$ in

15 in

6.G.2

2. There is a rectangular prism that is $7\frac{1}{2}$ cm wide. It has a height of $13\frac{1}{4}$ cm and a depth of 8 cm. What is its volume? Round to tenths.

6.G.2

3. Write an equation to represent the data shown in the chart below.

x	y
4.2	1.4
1.8	0.6
7.5	2.5

6.EE.9

4. What is the least common multiple of 6 and 10?

6.NS.4

5. How many twelfths are in $11\frac{1}{2}$?

6.NS.1

DAY 6
CHALLENGE
QUESTION

If there were SIX of the rectangular prisms from #1, what would be their total volume?

6.G.2

WEEK 20

ARGOPREP.COM

VIDEO EXPLANATIONS

Congratulations! You've made it to Week 20! This week you will study polygons on a coordinate plane to find lengths and answer real-world questions. You will also see nets that are a two-dimensional picture of a three-dimensional object. Finish strong!

You can find detailed video explanations to each problem in the book by visiting:
ArgoPrep.com

DAY I

When finding the volume of a cube, it is equal to (one side)³.

Use the figures below to answer questions 1 – 4.

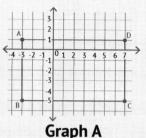

Graph A

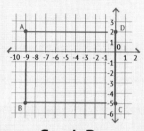

Graph B

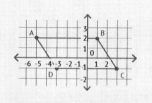

Graph C

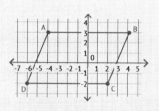

Graph D

---

1. Which graph above shows a shape with the coordinates below?

A (-9, 2)   B (-9, -5)   C (0, -5)   D (0, 2)

6.G.3

---

2. Which graph above shows a shape with the coordinates below?

A (-3, 1)   B (-3, -5)   C (7, -5)   D (7, 1)

6.G.3

---

3. Which graph above shows a shape with the coordinates below?

A (-5, 2)   B (1, 2)   C (3, -1)   D (-3, -1)

6.G.3

---

4. Which graph above shows a shape with the coordinates below?

A (-4, 3)   B (4, 3)   C (2, -2)   D (-6, -2)

6.G.3

Use the drawing below to answer questions 5 – 6.

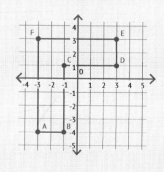

5. Which 2 sides have the same length?

6.G.3

6. What is the perimeter of the figure?

6.G.3

GPS works off of a grid-like system. You can use a coordinate system to determine direction.

DAY 2

Martin lives at the origin on the coordinate system below. Here are the locations of some buildings he might travel to:

Use the graph to answer questions 1 – 6.

Library	A	Max's house	D
School	B	Hospital	E
Store	C	Das Pizza Haus	F

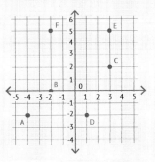

---

1. Martin wants to go see Max. What route can he take from his house Max's house?

6.G.3

---

2. After going to see Max, the boys decide to get pizza. What route could they take from Max's house?

6.G.3

---

3. After eating pizza, the boys needed to work on their projects at the library. What route can they take from Das Pizza Haus to the library?

6.G.3

---

4. From the library, the boys traveled 2 units up and 2 units right. Where did they go after the library?

6.G.3

---

5. In what quadrant is the hospital located?

6.NS.6

---

6. What is the distance between the library and the Max's house?

6.G.3

DAY 3

A net is formed when a three-dimensional object is "unfolded" and laid flat.

The net below is made of a square and 4 equal triangles. **Use the figure below to answer questions 1 – 2.**

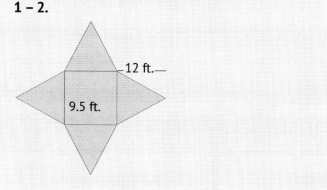

12 ft.

9.5 ft.

1. Which three-dimensional shape is formed by the figure to the left?

6.G.4

2. What is the surface area of the figure?

6.G.4

Use the figure below to answer questions 3 – 5.

7 in

7 in

3. Which three-dimensional shape is formed by the figure to the left?

6.G.4

4. What is the surface area of the figure?

6.G.4

5. What is the volume of the figure?

6.G.4

---

6. The rectangular prism below is made of cubes that have $\frac{1}{2}$-meter sides. What is the volume of the prism?

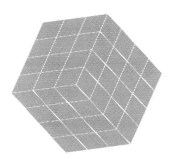

6.G.2

When looking at a net, consider how the shape might "fold" at the "joints" of the two-dimensional shape.

DAY 4

The figure below is measured in inches. **Use the figure to answer questions 1 – 3.**

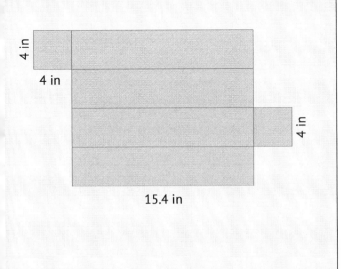

4 in

4 in

4 in

15.4 in

1. Which three-dimensional shape is formed by the figure?

6.G.4

2. What is the surface area of the figure?

6.G.4

3. What is the volume of the figure?

6.G.2

4. Which three-dimensional shape is formed by the figure below?

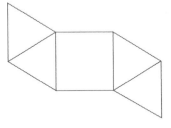

6.G.4

5. What is the greatest common factor of 41 and 43?

6.NS.4

6. What is the solution to this equation: $x - 5\frac{2}{3} = 9\frac{1}{2}$?

6.EE.7

Use the figure below to answer questions 1 – 3.

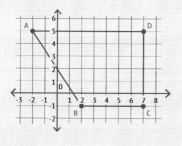

1. What is the area of the figure?

6.G.3

2. What is the distance between Points C and D?

6.NS.8

3. What is the distance between Points A and D?

6.NS.8

Use the figure below to answer questions 4 – 6.

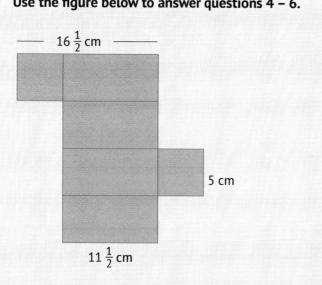

$16 \frac{1}{2}$ cm

5 cm

$11 \frac{1}{2}$ cm

4. Which three-dimensional shape is formed by the figure?

6.G.4

5. What is the volume of the figure?

6.G.2

6. What is the surface area of the figure?

6.G.4

DAY 6
CHALLENGE
QUESTION

What is the volume for the figure used in #1 - #3 if it were 8 units deep?

6.G.2

THE END!

:)

Assessment

ASSESSMENT

1. What is the area of the octagon?

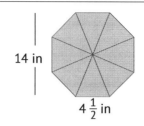

14 in

$4\frac{1}{2}$ in

6.G.1

Use the coordinate system below to answer questions 2 – 5.

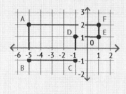

---

2. What is the y-coordinate of Point A?

6.NS.6

---

3. What point is located at (-1, 1)?

6.NS.6

---

4. What is the length of segment AF?

6.G.3

---

5. What is the perimeter for the above figure?

6.G.3

The chart below shows the scores for 4 of Penny's tests. **Use the table below to answer questions 6 – 7.**

Test	Score
A	87
B	92
C	83
D	88

6. Which test did Penny do the best on?

6.SP.5

7. Which test did Penny do the worst on?

6.SP.5

8. The rectangular prism below has a square base that measures 3 feet by 3 feet. What is the volume of the prism?

$11\frac{1}{2}$ ft.

6.G.2

9. What is the surface area of the rectangular prism shown in #8?

6.G.4

10. What is the value of $\frac{5}{6} \div \frac{2}{15}$?

6.NS.1

ASSESSMENT

Some couches were measured and their lengths are shown below.
Use this data to answer questions 11 – 12.

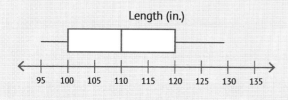

Length (in.)

95 100 105 110 115 120 125 130 135

11. What is the inter-quartile range (IQR) for the data set shown?

6.SP.3

12. What is the range for the data set shown?

6.SP.3

13. Renate has 497 beads. If it takes 27 beads per necklace, how many necklaces can Renate make?

6.NS.2

14. What is the value of the expression below when $m = -6$ and $n = 10$?

$-\dfrac{1}{2}m + n$

6.EE.2

15. Veronica earned $333 in 36 hours of work. How much money did she average per hour? Round your answer to the nearest cent.

6.NS.3

16. If Katelyn spent $918 on 12 pairs of pants, what was the cost of 1 pair?

6.RP.2

Shaun's credit card balance for 5 days was recorded and is shown below.
Use this information to answer questions 17.

Day	Balance ($)
1	– 18
2	492
3	– 119
4	890
5	250

17. Shaun wants to plot the balances on a number line. Which day will be the furthest to the left on the number line?

6.NS.7

18. What is another way to write $c + c + c + c + c + c$?

6.EE.3

19. What is the greatest common factor of 50 and 70?

6.NS.4

20. What is the solution to this equation: $b + 7.3 = 8$?

6.EE.7

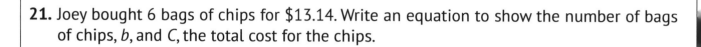

ASSESSMENT

21. Joey bought 6 bags of chips for $13.14. Write an equation to show the number of bags of chips, *b*, and *C*, the total cost for the chips.

6.EE.9

22. The temperature is 3.6°F. How would the temperature need to change so that the temperature is 0°F?

6.NS.5

23. What is 205% of 350?

6.RP.3

24. What is the GCF of 6, 12 and 24?

6.NS.4

25. 0.4 is what percent of 16?

6.RP.3

26. Forrest has $\frac{1}{4}$ of the money he needs to purchase a gift, *g*. If Forrest has $60, write an equation that could be used to find out how much money the gift costs.

6.EE.7

27. Write an equation that represents the data below.

x	y
2	3
4	5
6	7

6.EE.9

Ursula recorded her test scores and they are shown below. **Use this information to answer question 28.** Round your answer to the nearest hundredth.

Test scores:	82	94	85	78	92	88	80

28. What is the median of the data?

A. 17
B. 83
C. 85
D. 86

6.SP.2

29. Which of the following expressions is the same as $5(a - 7)$?

A. $2a + 3a + 5 - 7$
B. $3a - 3 - 2a - 4$
C. $5a - 35$
D. $4a - 7 + a$

6.EE.3

The data below represents the instruments musicians play. **Use this table to answer questions 30 – 31.**

Trumpet	24
Flute	16
Saxophone	18
Tuba	4

30. What is the ratio of trumpet players to saxophone players?

A. 1:6
B. 2:9
C. 3:4
D. 4:3

6.RP.1

31. What is the ratio of tuba players to flute players?

A. 1:4
B. 2:5
C. 4:1
D. 5:2

6.RP.1

32. Which data set is shown below?

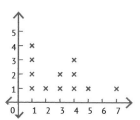

- **A.** 1, 4, 3, 3, 1, 7, 2, 4, 1, 5, 1, 4
- **B.** 1, 2, 3, 1, 4, 7, 5, 2, 5, 3, 1, 3
- **C.** 7, 2, 1, 3, 4, 1, 6, 1, 2, 4, 3, 5
- **D.** 2, 1, 1, 4, 3, 6, 7, 5, 3, 1, 4, 4

6.SP.4

---

33. It took Vanessa *m* minutes to dry her hair. William took 5 minutes less. How long did it take William to dry his hair?

- **A.** $m + 5$
- **B.** $m - 5$
- **C.** $5 - m$
- **D.** $5m$

6.EE.6

---

34. What is the least common multiple of 12 and 6?

- **A.** 2
- **B.** 3
- **C.** 6
- **D.** 12

6.NS.4

---

35. 72 is what percent of 360?

- **A.** 10%
- **B.** 12%
- **C.** 17%
- **D.** 20%

6.RP.3

---

36. What is the median of the data from #32?

- **A.** 2
- **B.** 3
- **C.** 4
- **D.** 5

6.SP.2

---

37. Which equation is true when *y* = 5?

- **A.** $-5 = -3y + 10$
- **B.** $5 = 3y + 10$
- **C.** $-3y = 10 - 5$
- **D.** $3y + 5 = 10$

6.EE.5

---

38. Which three-dimensional shape is formed by the figure below?

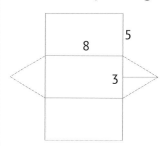

- **A.** rectangular prism
- **B.** triangular prism
- **C.** pyramid
- **D.** cube

6.G.4

39. What is the value of the expression below?

$3 + 10^3 \times 4$

A. 123
B. 2,704
C. 4,003
D. 8,788

6.EE.1

40. Which expression is equivalent to 11 (9 – 4)?

A. 99 – 44
B. 99 – 4
C. 20 – 15
D. 20 – 4

6.NS.4

41. Which two expressions are equivalent for any value of n?

A. 8 (n + 5) and 8n + 5
B. 8 (n – 1) and 8n – 8
C. 8 (8 – n) and 64 – n
D. 8n (n + 1) and 16n + 8n

6.EE.4

42. Which question below is a statistical question?

A. How many 6th grade teachers are at Springmore School?
B. Is your favorite teacher Mrs. Huston?
C. Which teachers do 6th graders like best?
D. Who is Nick's favorite teacher?

6.SP.1

43. To keep your heart healthy, it is recommended that you eat no more than 25 grams of fat per day. Which inequality shows how many fat grams, f, you can have and still be heart healthy?

A. $f \leq 25$
B. $f < 25$
C. $f > 25$
D. $f \geq 25$

6.EE.8

44. Tami owed $4,682. Which action will allow Tami to become debt-free?

A. Tami can pay $4,682 on her loan.
B. Tami can borrow $4,682 from her friend.
C. Tami can pay $4,000 on her loan.
D. Tami can spend $4,682.

6.NS.5

45. The coordinates of the vertices of a rectangle are A (-2, 4), B (0, 4), C (0, -3) and D (-2, -3). What are the dimensions of the rectangle?

A. 2 units by 7 units
B. 3 units by 4 units
C. 4 units by 2 units
D. 5 units by 7 units

6.NS.8

ANSWER
KEYS

VIDEO
EXPLANATIONS

ARGOPREP.COM

ANSWER KEYS

For more practice with 6th Grade Math, be sure to check out our other book
Argo Brothers Math Workbook Grade 6: Multiple Choice

WEEK 1

Day 1
1: $\frac{1}{2}$ km
2: $5\frac{1}{2}$ yards
3: $\frac{2}{9}$ cup
4: 14
5: $6\frac{1}{4} \div \frac{3}{4}$
6: $\frac{4}{9}$ yards

Day 2
1: $\frac{7}{8}$ km
2: 38
3: $\frac{2}{3}$ meters
4: $5\frac{1}{4} \div \frac{1}{2}$
5: $\frac{21}{22}$
6: $\frac{1}{4}$ cup

Day 3
1: $2\frac{5}{6} \div \frac{1}{3}$
2: $\frac{3}{4}$ meter
3: $2\frac{1}{5}$
4: $\frac{4}{5}$ yard
5: $2\frac{1}{4}$ inches
6: $3\frac{1}{2}$

Day 4
1: $2\frac{1}{3}$ miles
2: $10\frac{1}{2}$
3: $3\frac{1}{2}$
4: $16\frac{4}{5}$
5: $4\frac{1}{2} \div \frac{2}{3}$
6: 64

Day 5
1: 17
2: 13.5 inches
3: $10\frac{1}{2}$ yard
4: $3\frac{1}{4} \div \frac{1}{2}$
5: 28
6: 6 inches

Day 6
15

WEEK 2

Day 1
1: 208
2: 20
3: 70 r 2
4: 28
5: 21
6: 26

Day 2
1: 333
2: 175 r 3
3: 27
4: $11\frac{3}{4}$ inches
5: 60
6: 35

Day 3
1: 7.75
2: 42.78 cm
3: $71.28
4: 4
5: 23.3
6: 84 km

Day 4
1: 8.4 feet
2: 5.18 pounds
3: 42.3 miles
4: 221.5 miles
5: 1979.6 miles

Day 5
1: 396
2: 32
3: $5\frac{1}{2}$ meters
4: 34.2 pounds
5: 16.5 gallons
6: 214 miles

Day 6
63 inches

WEEK 3

Day 1
1: 23
2: 24
3: 30 minutes
4: 90 minutes
5: 20 minutes

Day 2
1: 25
2: $5\frac{1}{2}$
3: 24 hours
4: 7
5: 49.8 pounds
6: 36

Day 3
1: −5.1 cm
2: Deposit $143.78
3: $512
4: 44
5: 33
6: $4\frac{2}{5}$ feet

Day 4
1: +4.7°C
2: −615 meters
3: 28 + 14
4: $y = 71.3$
5: 42
6: $591.08

Day 5
1: $m = -91.3$
2: 20 days
3: 896 feet
4: 6
5: Pay $291
6: 90

Day 6
- 1605 yards

WEEK 4

Day 1
1: −3
2: A
3: 3
4: (1, 5)
5: Quadrant IV
6: 116

Day 2
1: Point B is a reflection of Point A, across the y–axis.
2: 4
3: − 4
4: (0, −2)
5: Quadrant II
6: (3, 5)

Day 3
1: #2
2: #5
3: #2
4: −1966 < 2106 or 2106 > −1966
5: $7\frac{1}{2}$ feet

Day 4
1: $|-11| > -7$
2: − 3
3: $|-5|$
4: −3
5: 396
6: $4\frac{3}{4} \div \frac{1}{2}$

Day 5
1: F
2: (− 2, − 4)
3: Point C
4: $-5.8 < |-\frac{14}{3}|$ or $|-\frac{14}{3}| > -5.8$
5: E
6: DCEBA

Day 6
Quadrant IV

WEEK 5

Day 1
1: 3 units by 11 units
2: E (3, −1), F (−2, 3)
3: 7 units
4: 7 units
5: 5 units by 6 units
6: 6 units

Day 2
1: 7 units by 4 units
2: 8
3: A (−5, 0), B (1, 4)
4: 8 units by 4 units
5: 32 units²
6: 24

Day 3
1: 203
2: 24
3: 34
4: 867
5: $-122\frac{1}{2}$
6: 24 minutes

Day 4
1: 888
2: − 44
3: 97
4: 188
5: −256
6: $-19\frac{3}{4}$

Day 5
1: 6 units
2: 4 units
3: 24 units²
4: − 32
5: 325.8
6: $g = -14.29$

Day 6
−82

WEEK 6

Day 1
1: 26
2: 35
3: 42
4: 21
5: (0, 2)
6: Point D

Day 2
1: 30
2: 9
3: 75
4: − 55
5: $|-\frac{5}{6}| > -|-\frac{5}{6}|$ or $-|-\frac{5}{6}| < |-\frac{5}{6}|$
6: Quadrant III

Day 3
1: −21
2: −15.8
3: −69
4: Test #5
5: Test 2 > Test 5 or Test 5 < Test 2

Day 4
1: $7y - 56$
2: $4d$
3: $50f - 30g$
4: $12b + 11$
5: (3, 4)
6: $a - 8$

Day 5
1: -52.6
2: 19.5
3: $30xy - 6xz$
4: $8(2c - 3d)$
5: $14.7x + 13.8y - 8$
6: $7m + 4n - 28$

Day 6
$16x - 23y + 26$

WEEK 7

Day 1
1: $4a$
2: $\frac{64}{125}$ cm³
3: 150 m²
4: $\frac{1}{64}$ ft³
5: 726 mm²
6: 77

Day 2
1: $216h^3$ units³
2: $2p + 3q$
3: $8(g + 2)$
4: 7 units by 4 units
5: 4 units
6: 248

Day 3
1: 181.5 in²
2: $5x + 100$
3: $\frac{27}{64}$ yd³
4: $(11b)^4$
5: $15ab - 33a$
6: 39

Day 4
1: $\frac{1}{27}$ ft³
2: $3w$
3: $600r^2$ cm²
4: c^3
5: $125w^3$ units³
6: 35

Day 5
1: 82.14 in²
2: $18z - 12$
3: $64e^3$ units³
4: $d - 5$
5: $n = 8.09$
6: Quadrant I

Day 6
$6s + 5t - 62$

WEEK 8

Day 1
1: $x = 4$
2: $y = 3$
3: $a = 1$
4: 8
5: $3x + 3$
6: 75.2°F

Day 2
1: $b = 5$
2: -14
3: $v = 8$
4: $r = 19$
5: $t \times t \times t \times t$
6: 48

Day 3
1: -5
2: 15
3: 3
4: 0, 2, 3
5: 2, 3
6: 213

Day 4
1: 12
2: $d = 12$
3: $k = \frac{1}{3}$
4: 0
5: $7w$
6: $5.19b$

Day 5
1: $j = 13$
2: $y = 8$
3: $21a$
4: 4
5: $j = 7$
6: $14.5 < |-15|$
or$| -15| > 14.5$

Day 6
$c + 8$

WEEK 9

Day 1
1: 16
2: $5g$
3: $s = \frac{1}{2}$
4: $d + 3$
5: $2d$
6: $d - 1$

Day 2
1: $18 - g$
2: $2m$
3: $p + 5$
4: $11p$ or $p(6 + 5)$
5: $\frac{1}{4} b$
6: 384 ft²

Day 3
1: $a - 4$
2: $3a$
3: $\frac{1}{4} a$
4: 3 units by 9 units
5: 9 units
6: 9

Day 4
1: $u = \frac{1}{3}$
2: $g - 15$
3: $\frac{1}{6} w$ feet
4: $m + 4$ feet
5: $\frac{1}{3} d$
6: $4n$

Day 5
1: $\frac{1}{2} d$ inches
2: $\frac{1}{2} d + 3$ inches
3: $p - 12$
4: $m + 1$ minutes
5: $\frac{5}{t}$
6: $512n^3$ units³

Day 6
Length: $11x$ cm
Perimeter: $44x$ cm

WEEK 10

Day 1
1: $5T = 27$
2: $5.40
3: $9h = 70.74$
4: $7.86
5: $w = 2.2$
6: $7 - y$

Day 2
1: $m - 9$ miles
2: 3 miles
3: $16 - m$ miles
4: $m + 2$ miles
5: $v = 5.4$
6: $b \leq 105$

Day 3
1: $l = 25$
2: $f \leq 12$
3: $e \geq 93$
4: $n \geq 17$
5: $c = 14.9$
6: $h > 20$

Day 4
1: $t = 48 \div 3$
2: $s = 60 \div 4$
3: $s > 9.35$
4: $e \leq 18$
5: $n < 33.25$
6: $8t - 4$

Day 5
1: $h \geq 9$
2: $w \leq 50$
3: 13
4: 77
5: $k = 18$
6: $4s = 96$

Day 6
$z \geq 4.5$

WEEK 11

Day 1
1: $y = \frac{1}{4} x$
2: $C = 25.2s$
3: $c = 95t$
4: $2s = b$ or $s = \frac{1}{2}b$
5: 2

Day 2
1: $s \geq 45$
2: $g = 14m$
3: $y = 1.5x$
4: 4, 5
5: $h - 5 \frac{1}{2}$

Day 3
1: 11:6
2: 2:3
3: 8:1
4: 22:1
5: 1:43

Day 4
1: 6:11
2: 4:9
3: 11:4
4: 3:7
5: $\frac{1}{3} j$

Day 5
1: 1:3
2: $y = \frac{4}{5} x$
3: $C = 1.15p$
4: 9
5: $y = 2x$

Day 6
15

WEEK 12

Day 1
1: $14
2: $\frac{4}{5}$ – ounce
3: $0.27/ounce
4: $0.13
5: $7.75
6: $\frac{1}{8}$ teaspoon

Day 2
1: $\frac{1}{2}$
2: $3.33
3: $1.12
4: $0.22/ounce
5: $2.49
6: $w \leq 500$

Day 3
1: 80
2: muenster cheese
3: roast beef
4: mozzarella & muenster
5: $12

Day 4
1: Irma
2: Jaxson
3: $4.53
4: $(12 - x)\, y$
5: $r = 5\frac{1}{2}$

Day 5
1: $6.80
2: $10.20
3: $1.35
4: 0.78 minutes
5: $y = 3x$

Day 6
413 miles

WEEK 13

Day 1
1: 92
2: 16.7%
3: 108
4: 140%
5: 5 units by 6 units
6: $\frac{7}{32}$ cups

Day 2
1: 28.2
2: 36
3: 33.3%
4: 84
5: $15\frac{1}{2}$
6: 117

Day 3
1: 2 hours
2: 9
3: 36
4: 525
5: $\frac{1}{3} k$

Day 4
1: The response can be only 1 number.
2: The response can only be yes or no.
3: The response can be only 1 number.
4: The response can be only 1 number.
5: 66
6: 1:4

Day 5
1: 20 km
2: 6
3: 20%
4: The response can be only yes or no.
5: 3

Day 6
Any question that samples more than 1 person/thing and has a range of possible answers is a statistical question.

WEEK 14

Day 1
1: 79
2: 8
3: 79.57
4: 1 day
5: 1.9
6: 4

Day 2
1: 5
2: 6.5
3: 6.5
4: $0.50
5: $5(5k - 2)$

Day 3
1: 23
2: 32.5
3: 32.9
4: 103
5: $C = 4.5b$

Day 4
1: 27
2: 17.5
3: 15.8
4: 5, 23
5: 24

Day 5
1: 42
2: 22.5
3: 25.8
4: median
5: $y = \frac{1}{5} x$

Day 6
28.3

WEEK 15

Day 1
: 58
: 14
: 9
: The response can be only 1 number.
: Deposit $294.07
: 12.5%

Day 2
1: 15
2: 30
3: 110
4: 78
5: 8 units
6: 26 units

Day 3
1: 18
2: 13
3: 9
4: 14
5: 1:12
6: 17

Day 4
1: 80
2: 10
3: 24
4: 78 meters
5: 8 units
6: 8 units

Day 5
1: 25
2: 89.8
3: 90.5
4: 72
5: 111%
6: 24 minutes

Day 6
12

WEEK 16

Day 1
1: Table D
2: Table B
3: Table C
4: Table A
5:

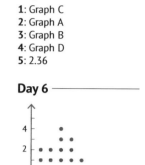

Day 2
1: Data C
2: Data B
3: Data D
4: Data C
5: 0.5

Day 3
1: Graph B
2: Graph D
3: Graph A
4: Graph C
5: $m = (\frac{5}{12})b$

Day 4
1: Table D
2: Table C
3: Table B
4: Table A
5: 355

Day 5
1: Graph C
2: Graph A
3: Graph B
4: Graph D
5: 2.36

Day 6

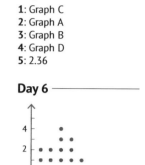

WEEK 17

Day 1
1: 144
2: Lena
3: Paula & Daisy
4: $M - 18$
5: 0, 2, 3, 5
6: 0.21

Day 1
1: 7
2: 4
3: 20
4: 3
5: 73
6: 12 feet

Day 3
1: blue
2: 100
3: 15
4: 45
5: 3:1
6: 1:4

Day 4
1: 1
2: 7
3: 25
4: 75
5: 3
6: 3

Day 5
1: tofu
2: chicken
3: beef
4: pork & turkey
5: 1:1
6: 20:7

Day 6
100

WEEK 18

Day 1
1: 30 cm²
2: 80 cm²
3: 63 in²
4: 28.4 m²
5: 130
6: 8

Day 1
1: 34.1 in²
2: 169 in²
3: $37\frac{3}{8}$ ft²
4: 85.5 in²
5: $y = 2x$
6: 276 cm²

Day 3
1: 64 cm²
2: 20 cm²
3: 16 cm²
4: 18 cm²
5: 118 cm²
6: −3, 0, 1

Day 4
1: 73.5 in²
2: 30.25 yds²
3: 54 in²
4: $\frac{8}{35}$ m²
5: 56
6: $c > 100$

Day 5
1: 32 m²
2: 48 m²
3: 161 m²
4: 81 mm²
5: $d = 14\frac{1}{4}$
6: −10

Day 6
8.1 mm²

WEEK 19

Day 1
1: 300.6 in³
2: 3.3 cm³
3: 448.14 cm³
4: 106.75 mm³
5: $\frac{3}{8}$ − quart
6: 56.55

Day 2
1: 762.5 m³
2: 16 m³
3: 2 in²
4: $1\frac{1}{3}$ cm³
5: 7 units by 5 units
6: 114

Day 3
1: $13\frac{1}{2}$ yards³
2: 1,025 in³
3: 306 ft³
4: $\frac{8}{9}$ in³
5: 351 cm³
6: 3

Day 4
1: 551.4 m³
2: 819 cm³
3: 14:9
4: 7:8
5: 4:3

Day 5
1: $426\frac{2}{3}$ in³
2: 795 cm³
3: $y = \frac{1}{3}x$
4: 30
5: 138

Day 6
2,560 in³

WEEK 20

Day 1
1: B
2: A
3: C
4: D
5: ED and AB
6: 26 units

Day 2
1: go right 1 unit, then down 2 units
2: go 7 units up and 3 units left
3: go 7 units down and 2 units left
4: school
5: Quadrant I
6: 5 units

Day 3
1: pyramid
2: 318.25ft^2
3: cube
4: 294 in^2
5: 343 in^3
6: 6 m^3

Day 4
1: rectangular prism
2: 278.4 in^2
3: 246.4 in^3
4: pyramid
5: 1
6: $x = 15\frac{1}{6}$

Day 5
1: 42 units^2
2: 6 units
3: 9 units
4: rectangular prism
5: 287.5 cm^3
6: 280 cm^2

Day 6
336 units^3

End of Year Assessment

1: 126 in^2
2: 2
3: D
4: 6 units
5: 18 units
6: Test B
7: Test C
8: 103.5 ft^3
9: 156 ft^2
10: $6\frac{1}{4}$
11: 20
12: 35
13: 18
14: 13
15: $9.25

16: $76.50
17: Day 3
18: $6c$
19: 10
20: $b = 0.7$
21: $C = 2.19b$
22: $-3.6°F$
23: 717.5
24: 6
25: 2.5%
26: $\frac{1}{4}g = 60$
27: $y = x + 1$
28: C
29: C
30: D

31: A
32: A
33: B
34: D
35: D
36: B
37: A
38: B
39: C
40: A
41: B
42: C
43: A
44: A
45: A

Made in the USA
Lexington, KY
21 March 2018